T0114662

SOLVING THE MYSTERY OF THE
REDOUBLE

James Marsh Sternberg, MD (Dr J)

and

Danny Kleinman

authorHOUSE

AuthorHouse™
1663 Liberty Drive
Bloomington, IN 47403
www.authorhouse.com
Phone: 833-262-8899

Published by AuthorHouse 05/2023

ISBN: 979-8-8230-0537-1 (sc)
ISBN: 979-8-8230-0536-4 (e)

Also by James Marsh Sternberg

Playing to Trick One – No Mulligans in Bridge (Second Edition)

Trump Suit Headaches; Rx for Declarers and Defenders

The Finesse; Only a Last Resort

Blocking and Unblocking

Shortness – a Key to Better Bidding (Second Edition)

When Michaels Met the Unusual

From Zero to Three Hundred; A Bridge Journey

Reversing the Dummy

Trump Promotion; The Uppercut

Active or Passive – Becoming a Better Defender

James Marsh Sternberg with Danny Kleinman

Second Hand High; Third Hand Not So High

An Entry, An Entry, My Kingdom For An Entry

L O L; Loser on Loser

In Search of a Second Suit

Elimination and Endplay

Suit Preference; Abused and Misused

Solving the Mystery of the Redouble

DEDICATION

To

VICKIE LEE BADER

In appreciation of her love and devotion

for so many years

J M S

To my bridge friends and partners from long ago, dead or living:

Judy Abrams   Susan Alch   Harold Anderson   Jo Anderson

Arthur Auer   Mark Bartusek   Marvyne Betsch   Ronnie Blau

Alan Brody   Pedro Cabral   Claude W. Cain III   Vicki Colvin

Ward Corbin   Bill DeForest   Rose Eidem   Billy Eisenberg

Mike Engel   Bobbi Erde   Laurie Gaskins   Mike Gilbert

Norman Gore   Fred Hamilton   Bob Hamman   Alyce Harris

Lyndon Henry   Norbert Jay   Diane Jonas   Barbara Kachmar

Eddie Kantar   Dave Kitzes   Carl Klaus   Richard Love

Walter May   Diane Mayer   Bill McWilliams   Patti Medford

Marshall Miles   Jock Millenson   Joe Norris   June E. Osborn

Jim Phillips   Gene Prosnitz   Mike Raphael   Dick Recht

Jeff Rubens   George Sagarin   Dennis Stone   Paul Trent

Fran Tsacnaris   Noreen Walsh   Jim Watson   Larry Weiss

--- D M K

ACKNOWLEDGEMENTS

This book would not have been possible without the help of several friends. Michael Lawrence, Anne Lund, Frank Stewart and especially Karen Walker all provided suggestions for material for this book.

Jim is forever indebted to Hall of Famer Fred Hamilton, the late Allan Cokin and Bernie Chazen, without whose guidance and teaching he would not have achieved whatever success he has had in bridge.

Special thanks to our editor Willie Fuchs for his keen eye and suggestions.

James Marsh Sternberg, MD
Palm Beach Gardens, FL
mmay001@aol.com

Danny Kleinman
Los Angeles, CA
dannyk13@ca.rr.com

CHAPTERS

1. Introduction 1

2. Scoring Redoubled Contracts 7

3. Getting Started, Deals 1 - 3 10

4. A Side Note 22

5. Advancer's Calls After Responder Redoubles, Deals 4 – 7 27

6. Opener's Rebid When Responder Redoubles, Deal 8 39

7. Responder's Rebid Options, Deals 9 - 10....................................46

8. Redoubles After We Find A Fit, Deal 11 52

9. SOS Redoubles, Deals 12 - 15 57

10. Redoubles After Doubles Of Artificial Bids, Deal 16 70

11. The Big Swing 84

12. Redoubles After The Opponents Open, Deal 17.........................88

13. Redoubles After Their Notrumps And Ours 91

14. Other Redoubles...95

      Rosenkranz Redoubles 96

      Support Redoubles, Deal 18 97

      'Bop' Doubles 99

      Some New Tricks.. 101

      The Scrambling Redouble 103

      The Striped–Tail Ape, Deal 19 104

15. Additional Deals 20 – 32.. 106

Redouble? First, you probably need to blow the dust off your redouble bidding card since it's been sitting unused in your bidding box for so long that it has mold and dust on it. Some of you may not even be able to find it. Hint: it's purple with two big XX's on it.

When we get asked, and we rarely do, what does redouble mean, we respond as follows. A redouble is usually an either-or bid. By that we mean it usually has one of two meanings. One is a desire to subsequently penalize the opponents, the other is a limit raise or better of partner's suit without maximum trump support. In a major that would be four pieces, in a minor usually five.

Sounds simple? Yes, but like everything in bridge, you have to dig deeper. There are three other players at the table. Two opponents and hopefully a helpful partner. Now everything depends on what happens next which is what this book is all about. The bidding is just getting started. And remember, we said usually, not always. Ready? Let's go!

CHAPTER ONE

INTRODUCTION

Because we seldom use them, redoubles are little explored and discussed in bridge literature. They remain thorny for most players. Ask yourself: when was the last time you redoubled? Chances are that even then you had a better call at the time.

To make sense of the discussions that follow, you will do well to understand what 'natural' means in bridge. Here is a definition:

Natural

A call, showing a desire or willingness to play in the bid or last-bid strain, at its current level or higher, without saying anything about another strain.

No call is natural if it provides information about strains other than the last named strain, except by inference from previous or omitted calls. Otherwise:

A bid that suggests playing in the named strain is natural.

A double that suggests defending against the bid doubled is natural.

A redouble that suggests playing in the redoubled contract is natural.

Any pass that denies values is natural. Any pass that follows a pass by RHO is natural if it suggests playing in the current contract. Any pass that follows a bid, double or redouble by RHO is natural if its only message is "nothing to say at this time" and neither promises nor denies values.

Calls that are not natural are *artificial.* These fall into several categories.

Some are *descriptive* of suit lengths. Think of a 4♣ response to 1♡ when played as most now do, a splinter raise. It describes the bidder's heart length of four or more, and unless defined more specifically, 'shortness' in clubs.

Some are strength-showing like an Omnibus 2♣ when played as the only forcing opening. Some are strength-denying like the Heart Murmur, a conventional 2♡ response to that 2♣ opening that denies having as much as a king.

Some are *neutral* like the usual 2◊ response to 2♣ that denies only the partnership's requirements for a positive response.

Some are *queries* such as a Stayman 2♣ or a Blackwood 4NT. Others are *replies* like a *natural* 2♡ reply to a Stayman 2♣ or a *coded* 5♡ reply to a Blackwood 4NT.

Others are *surrogates,* such as a Stayman user's Smolen 3♠ rebid that shows five hearts after opener has denied a four-card major.

Then there are *transfers,* such as a Jacoby Transfer 3♡ response to 2NT, *puppets* like a "Lebensohl" 2NT response to 1NT after an opposing 2♠ overcall, or *marionettes* like a "Lebensohl" 2NT advance of a takeout double of an opposing Weak 2♠ Bid.

Some are *preludes* like a "Hamilton" 2♣ overcall of an opposing 1NT opening. Overcaller's next call over advancer's usual *neutral* 2◊ reply will then reveal which of the four suits he has.

Some are *cultural.* Think of a 2♣ response to 1NT. It had a natural meaning, "Let's play in two clubs," but after the widespread adoption of Stayman it acquired a cultural meaning: "I'd like to find a major-suit fit." Likewise, a 2NT jump overcall of a 1♡ opening had a natural meaning, "I would have opened two notrump had nobody opened ahead of me," but thanks to Al Roth's invention of 'Unusual 2NT Overcalls,' it eventually acquired the cultural meaning, 'Two lowest unbid suits.'

Doubles of opening suit bids were played as natural ("I can beat you!") until even before contract bridge replaced auction, Bryant McCampbell suggested that it should be played otherwise.

Though penalty doubles of suit openings disappeared by the time Danny first played bridge, takeout doubles hadn't yet replaced them. Though intended to be taken out, the 'informatory doubles' popular for a few decades said only "I have opening-bid values."

As late as 1962, 'Good hand' was the cultural meaning of doubles of suit openings until a new generation of players adopted the modern cultural meaning of takeout doubles championed by Edgar Kaplan.

Starting in 1967, more and more players abandoned natural 'business' (penalty) doubles for the much more useful *Sputnik* (now called 'Negative') Doubles, a new cultural meaning popularized by Al Roth.

Under rules intended to last, the artificial calls we have called cultural would be alertable, a way to tell opponents "this call does not mean what at first glance you might suppose it does, so you'd better examine our convention card or ask me to explain."

But under rules that change every decade, calls with cultural meanings no longer require alerts. Thus unless alerted, a 2♣ response to 1NT asks for a four-card major and normally promises at least one. Likewise, a 2NT overcall of a 1♡ opening shows both minors, and most significantly for our purposes here, doubles of suit openings are no longer for penalties.

As *cultural* meanings of many doubles have replaced their natural meanings, so also cultural meanings of redoubles have replaced their natural meanings.

Harold Vanderbilt invented the redouble in 1925. "Sending it back", a slang term for redoubling, was intended to quadruple the score. That's its natural meaning. But over time, just as with many penalty doubles, more useful cultural meanings were found for redoubles.

Commonly found in the bridge literature is the teaching that if partner opens the bidding and the next player makes a takeout double, responder should redouble 'to show 10 or more high-card points' ('HCP'). That usually ends the discussion of redoubles. We'll discuss when such redoubles are a good idea and when not.

Unless partner has already shown defensive strength, low-level penalty doubles are seldom profitable. This has led to a tsunami of artificial or conventional doubles: negative, maximal, je ne sais quoi, you name it. Still, some penalty doubles must remain to deter opponents from disruptive wild preempts and cheap undoubled saves.

The advent of takeout doubles and other artificial doubles required and led to artificial redoubles.

'Business' redoubles are less useful than business doubles, especially at duplicate bridge. We have another name for 'business' redoubles, which we'll use in the rest of this book: *Greedy Redoubles*. With apologies to Gordon Gekko, we'll affirm 'Greed is good.' Sometimes---but not often. But in the absence of a clear understanding, Greedy Redoubles are the default.

Making a doubled contract figures to earn you a near top. If you redouble you may scare the opponents into running, snatching a tepid result from the jaws of victory. So let's see what has been done to put redoubles to better use than greed. Bear in mind there are two kinds of information to exchange: (1) suits and shape and (2) strength. But when you show your suits, you also imply the strength to do so at the level required.

One simple way to understand responder's redoubles is the following: redoubles *anchor* the hand by saying, "This deal belongs to our side. We have the balance of high-card strength." That is the *cultural* meaning of a redouble of 1♡-double-redouble.

Typically, responder hopes to double the opponents' runout for penalties, and indeed his redouble triggers penalty doubling by either partner. We call such redoubles *anchor* redoubles. Usually responder hungers for the opponents' blood, so we may call those doubles *vampire* redoubles. All subsequent doubles by either partner are for penalty. But responder does not always seek to double the opponents at a low level.

Sometimes responder redoubles to show a game-invitational or stronger raise with specifically three-card support for opener's major or four-card support for his minor. Even if you play a 1NT response to a major as forcing and perhaps a prelude to a delayed raise to three, 1NT is natural and non-forcing over an intervening takeout double. So some of your anchor redoubles are *fit*, but not too great a fit, redoubles.

Likewise, even though you play two-over-one responses as forcing, whether for one round or to game, these responses are natural and completely non-forcing over an intervening takeout double. So redoubles change subsequent new-suit responses from non-forcing to *forcing*. We may call such redoubles *oomph* redoubles. Responder's next call will normally clarify his redouble as either a fit redouble, oomph redouble, or *vampire* redouble.

If you redouble and raise opener's suit next, your redouble is a fit redouble, forcing if you jump, invitational if you don't, showing secondary support. If you redouble and bid notrump or a new suit next, your redouble is an oomph redouble, showing a stronger hand than a direct response in that strain. If you redouble and double the opponent's runout next, your redouble is a vampire redouble, thirsting for the opponents' blood.

"But at my back I always hear Time's winged chariot hurrying near"
---Andrew Marvell (To His Coy Mistress)

It's equally important to understand when *not* to redouble. When you have 10 HCP or more and your RHO has made a takeout double, you have to be thinking ahead to your next call. Do you have a hand for an oomph redouble? Perhaps you should bid your suit instead.

It's useful to play that after an opposing takeout double, a new-suit response is forcing at the one-level but not the two-level. Why so? Because only at the one-level does opener have a cheap, convenient 1NT rebid available. Plan your auction.

Suppose your partner opens 1◊ and your RHO doubles. You start to drool, as you have 11 HCP with a 5=4=2=2 hand pattern. You can hope to nail the opponents for a juicy penalty in 1♡ doubled and a juicier penalty still in 1♠ doubled. So you redouble.

Oops! That nasty Lefty jumps to 3♣. As we will reiterate later, Lefty's jump does not show 11 HCP. Not unless you're playing with a 44-HCP deck. He's trying to shut you and your partner out. Who does he think he is, Sandy Koufax? But when his weak preempt comes round to you, you realize he's succeeded. Even if you're Henry Aaron. When you see that fastball down the middle, take your best swing at it. Don't wait for a 2-2 count, when you may face Sandy's best curve.

CHAPTER TWO

SCORING

REDOUBLED

CONTRACTS

SCORING   REDOUBLED   CONTRACTS

When Harold Vanderbilt invented them in 1925, redoubles were intended to quadruple the score. Let's review the scoring.

UNDERTRICKS:

Non-vul	Undoubled	Doubled	Redoubled
Down 1	-50	-100	-200
Down 2	-100	-300	-600
Down 3	-150	-500	-1000
Down 4	-200	-800	-1600

Vulnerable	Undoubled	Doubled	Redoubled
Down 1	-100	-200	-400
Down 2	-200	-500	-1000
Down 3	-300	-800	-1600

MAKING REDOUBLED CONTRACTS

(a) The trick score, majors 30, minors 20, notrumps 40 for first trick and 30 for all others is quadrupled.

(b) If the trick score is at least 100, a game bonus of 300 (non-vul) or 500 (vulnerable) is added.

(c) A redoubled bonus of 100 is added.

(d) A bonus for each overtrick: 200 (non-vul) or 400 (vulnerable) is added.

Example: 1♡ redoubled, vulnerable, making two

Trick score:	4 x 30 = 120	(a)
Game bonus:	= 500	(b)
Redoubled bonus:	= 100	(c)
One overtrick:	= 400	(d)
	Total: +1120	

In modern bidding, the use of redoubles at low levels has increased greatly. We'll discuss the various uses in depth.

However, prior to 1987 an interesting scoring anomaly brought about some strange scoring situations, especially at high levels.

Until then, making a doubled *or redoubled* contract earned only a 50-point bonus 'for insult'. For example, making a non-vulnerable 5◊ redoubled with an overtrick earned 950---20 points *more* than the 920 for bidding and making 6◊.

By contrast, making a vulnerable 5◊ redoubled with an overtrick earned 1350---20 points *less* than the 1370 for bidding and making 6◊. The Striped-Tail Ape (you'll meet him later) could sit in his tree grinning instead of fleeing.

A scoring change in the 1987 *Law*s increased the bonus for making a redoubled contract to 100 points and sparked protests in the forest.

CHAPTER THREE

GETTING

STARTED

DEALS 1 - 3

The most common redouble is responder's redouble of a doubled suit opening. This redouble promises at least 10 HCP and tells opener "It's our hand."

Unless opener has made an opening on shape with 5-5 or 6-4 in two suits and only 10 HCP (we don't condone one-bids with less than 10 HCP), your side has more than half the high-card strength in the deck. Your redouble usually shows a desire to penalize opposing runouts or is a prelude to showing an invitational or better raise of opener's suit *with less than primary* support.

On occasion, it's a prelude to showing a hand that would otherwise have started with a strong two-over-one response.

A redouble followed by a raise of partner's major-suit opening denies four-card support, for which an artificial 2NT jump, a convention called 'Jordan' is available.

After a minor-suit opening, a redouble followed by a raise denies five-card support, for which "Jordan," "Criss-Cross," "TWIT" or other conventions are available.

Why? Silkwood's Law says: "When you have a story that needs telling, tell it now. You may not get another chance." Primary support for partner's suit is always a story worth telling, and when that suit is a major, it's the most important story.

A redouble after a take-out double of a suit opening creates a forcing auction. Responder's redouble promises at least one more bid---except when either partner doubles an opponent's runout. The opponents must run unless they play penalty passes of redoubles. Some pairs do so when the redoubled opening is 1♣ or 1◊, a rare treatment that they must alert. Any following doubles by responder or opener are for penalty. Many large penalties---300 points, 500 points or more are available for doubling their runouts, even at low levels. Compare these to doubles of voluntarily bid games, which rarely go down more than one or two.

If redoubler's next call is in opener's suit at the lowest level, it shows an invitational three-card limit raise of a major (four-card limit raise of a minor). To show a forcing raise, redoubler must jump or cue bid.

We can extend this technique. Suppose partner has overcalled and your right-hand opponent makes a Negative Double. Let's put that double to our advantage, using the same principle.

Lefty	Partner	Righty	You	
1♣ or 1♦	1♡ or 1♠	Double*	?	*Negative

Choices include:

Raises of overcaller's major, with jump raises serving as weak preempts.

Redouble, showing a strong hand while denying four-card support for overcaller's major, and often hoping to penalize the opponents.

2NT, a la Jordan, showing a four-card limit raise or better.

If you would otherwise use two of opener's minor as a cue-bid to show whatever else it might show in the absence of the Negative Double, as a bonus, you may now want to play it as natural. Another option is a single raise with 3 better trumps.

Abandon the Greedy Redouble in this auction? Yes, here and in many other auctions. Sometimes all a redouble accomplishes is to let opener off the hook and let responder pick a safe landing place.

Even before the modern era, when doubles of overcalls were used as penalty doubles, most Greedy Redoubles of low-level overcalls were less than useless. They often warned the opponents to run when the overcall was about to make, and merely gilded the lily when the opponents sat for them. We'll discuss later when we still need them.

Probably other than the cards for seven-bids, redouble cards are the least-used cards in your bidding box.

To protect the reputations of the guilty (except his own), we've changed the names in this story from Danny's vast rubber-bridge past.

The year was 1970 and Danny was playing at the short-lived Continental Bridge Club near the famous Chasen's restaurant. He had cut as his partner a woman we'll call 'Miss Guggenheim', a name very familiar to readers of S.J. Simon's books.

At penny-a-point stakes when they could still buy steaks at Chasen's, Danny and Miss Guggenheim were vulnerable. Examine this deal:

Danny (Dummy)
♠ A J 8
♡ A
♢ J 10
♣ K Q J 8 7 3 2

Futile Willie
♠ K 10 7 4
♡ K J 6 5 2
♢ 9 8 6
♣ 5

Mr. Smug
♠ 2
♡ 10 9 4
♢ A K Q 7 5 4 3 2
♣ 6

Miss Guggenheim
♠ Q 9 6 5 3
♡ Q 8 7 3
♢ Void
♣ A 10 9 4

Danny	Mr. Smug	Miss Guggenheim	Futile Willie
1♣	5♢	5♠	Dbl
Redbl	All	Pass	

Miss G ruffed the ♢Q at Trick 1 and finessed the ♠J. Mr. Smug followed with the ♠2. Flushed with success, Miss G returned to her hand by ruffing a second diamond and continued with the ♠Q. Willie covered with the ♠K. Miss G won dummy's ♠A and led to her ♠9 to draw the last trump.

Oops, did we say 'the' last trump? Actually it was *her* last trump. Willie won the ♠10 and led his last diamond. Mr. Smug showed his hand and said, "We get the rest."

"No you don't," said Miss G. "I still get dummy's ace of hearts at Trick 13 when you're through running diamonds."

"Actually, not," said Willie. "By then, I'll have pitched all my hearts and I still have a trump left. I'm a genius!"

Miss G conceded the rest graciously, throwing her cards in. Willie and Mr. Smug threw their cards in over hers. As Danny struggled in vain to separate the cards jumbled in the middle of the table, Miss G jumped up from her chair and ran to the table where the Unlucky Expert, her current boyfriend, was playing a set game with her mother against two self-styled hotshots.

Forty seconds later, she returned crying, "Henry says your redouble was a business redouble."

"Yes, it was," said Danny. "Why didn't you make an overtrick?"

Willie's double had tipped off the winning line: ♠Q at Trick 2, covered by the ♠K and ♠A, club to the ♣A, finesse the ♠8, cash dummy's ♠J and then claim six, saying "Running clubs until you ruff in."

Lesson: Don't redouble contracts that your *partner* is apt to butcher.

The Official Encyclopedia of Bridge shows a Greedy Redouble at its best:

North	East	South	West	
1♣	P	2♡*	P	*Strong jump shift
2NT	P	6♡	P	
P	Dbl	?		

South holds ♠ AJ2 ♡ AKQ8642 ◊ K95 ♣ void

East's double, calling for an unusual lead, usually dummy's first suit, is likely based on the ♣AK or ♣AQ. East is unlikely to be void in clubs but if he is, South can overruff.

South should redouble.

WEIGHING ALTERNATIVES AND PLANNING AHEAD

Must you always redouble your partner's garden-variety suit opening with 10 or more HCP after RHO's takeout double? No, despite what all too often we hear. As in all other auctions, you must *weigh your alternatives* and *plan ahead*.

Your alternatives include natural bids, raises and jump raises, one-level responses, two-level responses in lower-ranking suits, jump shifts, conventional raises, and *passes*.

Why should you ever want to pass with a good hand? Doesn't Silkwood's Law warn you to tell your story while you still can?

Yes, but there's one story you cannot tell by bidding or redoubling: an *extreme* desire to defend. Bidding anything takes your opponents off the hook. Redoubling takes advancer, the doubler's partner, off the hook, and may also take the doubler off the hook if opener bids ahead of him.

As we'll see later, opener won't always pass if you redouble. With good shape, assured of your 10 or more high-card points, he might bid instead of giving you a chance to double the opponent's runout to his short suit.

Here are a pair of hands that we shall call the *Spider* and the *Fly*. Actually, there are many such pairs of hands. Here are a Heart Spider and Heart Fly:

You, responder, hold ♠ KQ109 ♡ 2 ◊ KQ109 ♣ KQ109, a Heart Spider, and Lefty, advancer, holds ♠ 432 ♡ 76543 ◊ 32 ♣ 432, a Heart Fly. Righty doubles your partner's 1♡ opening.

What do you think will happen if you redouble? Lefty is off the hook. Partner may have shape and bid. Now Righty is off the hook too.

But if you pass, Lefty is still on the hook, and if he bids 1♠ (what else?), Righty may even raise. When you double now, it's a Killer Double.

This is an extreme case of the Spider and the Fly ("Come into my parlor," said the Spider to the Fly), but there are enough hands like it to make pass-then-double an option for responder with a strong misfitting hand.

Plan your auction. If you redouble, what do you plan to do at your next turn? After

Partner	Righty	You	Lefty
1♡	Dbl	Redbl	2♣
P	P	?	

… Your options include:

2♡, a three-card limit raise, letting partner stop at the two-level.

3♡, a three-card forcing to game raise.

Double, 100% intended for penalties.

Pass, FORCING. They bid the one suit I can't double, can you?

2◊, 2♠, 3◊, 3♠, new suits or a 3♣ cue bid, all forcing.

2NT game-invitational or 3NT, let's play here.

4NT Natural and slam-invitational.

If none of these options appeal to you, maybe you should have bid something else the first time instead of redoubling. In the modern style, you can bid a new suit at the one-level to force for at least one round.

We recommend treating new suits at the one-level as forcing, but we do not recommend the modern treatment of responder's single-jump shifts as weak preempts; they are too valuable as natural and invitational with good six-card suits.

Weak single-jumps no longer scare today's opponents. If anything, your jumps goad them into bidding more. When you are weak, their finesses are working and they often make what they bid.

Invitational jumps are just as preemptive as weak jumps. They consume just as much bidding space, but they are preempts with *teeth*. If the opponents sell out, you make. If they bid on, they'll get overboard and they'll often get nailed with penalty doubles.

Silkwood's Law again: "When you have a story that needs telling, tell it now. You may not get another chance." And when you do get another chance, you can tell a second story.

You hold ♠ 8 ♡ AJ643 ◊ QJ5 ♣ K975 when the bidding starts:

Partner	Righty	You	Lefty
1♣	Dbl	?	

Too often we hear "But partner, I had to redouble, I had 11 HCP."

16

If you redouble, Lefty may jump to 2♠, which most play as a weak preempt, or 3♠, which all play as a weak preempt. What then?

Help !! Wouldn't you be happier after:

Partner	Righty	You	Lefty
1♣	Dbl	1♡	2♠
P	P	3♣	

You don't need a five-card suit to bid at the one-level. Just as you would had Righty passed, you can bid a four-card major that you'd be happy for partner to raise with four or high-honor third and a ruffing value.

After Righty doubles partner's 1◊ opening, make your normal 1♡ response with ♠ 74 ♡ QJ52 ◊ K64 ♣ J1083. You don't want to face:

Partner	Righty	You	Lefty
1◊	Dbl	P	1♠
P	P	?	

Respond 1♡ also with ♠ 74 ♡ AQ52 ◊ K64 ♣ J1083, despite your 10 HCP. You don't want to face:

Partner	Righty	You	Lefty	
1◊	Dbl	Redbl*	1♠	* I got points, Pard!"
P	P	?		

Bid your *suits* while you can before the auction gets too high.

In days of old, bridge authorities taught that no suit response was forcing over an intervening takeout double. Not a good way to play! We can afford to play a new suit as forcing when opener can rebid cheaply, e.g. 1NT with a balanced minimum.

Opener may not have such a convenient rebid available over a new suit at the two-level. So it's still best to play a response of two of a new suit as non-forcing over a takeout double, requiring little more than a good suit, playable opposite a low doubleton.

After 1♥ - Dbl, bid 2♣ with ♠ 64 ♥ 93 ♦ Q43 ♣ KJ10642. It's neither forcing nor especially encouraging, but precisely because partner may pass, you do need a *good suit*. Add an ace or king, and if you play invitational jump shifts as we favor, you can bid 1♥ - double - 3♣ with ♠ 64 ♥ 93 ♦ QJ4 ♣ AKJ1053 or

♠ A4 ♥ 93 ♦ Q43 ♣ KJ10642   or   ♠ 64 ♥ K3 ♦ Q43 ♣ KJ10642.

But with a stronger hand still, e.g. ♠ A6 ♥ K3 ♦ Q43 ♣ KJ10642, you can afford to redouble now and bid clubs later, forcing, e.g.:

1♥	Dbl	Redbl	P	or	1♥	Dbl	Redbl	2♠
P	1♠	2♣			P	P	3♣	

Deal # 1   Redouble or What?

Vul: N/S   ♠ 6 5
                           ♡ A J 6
                           ◊ K J 5 4 3
                           ♣ K J 3

♠ K J 10 8 7 3   ♠ A Q 9 4
♡ 5 2   ♡ 10 9 4
◊ 9 8 6   ◊ Q 7
♣ 9 5   ♣ A 8 6 4

                           ♠ 2
                           ♡ K Q 8 7 3
                           ◊ A 10 2
                           ♣ Q 10 7 2

North	East	South	West
1◊	Dbl	Redbl	3♠
P	P	?	

What should South do now? Double? Obviously North and South have the majority of the high cards.

This is a typical example of the "I've ten or more high-card points" redouble without thinking about one's next call. How could South avoid this headache?

South should respond naturally. Look how much better placed he is after:

North	East	South	West
1◊	Dbl	1♡	3♠
P	P	4◊	P
4♡	?	?	

East will likely save in 4♠ (perhaps he should have bid it directly). But if so, with fits in both red suits and a singleton spade, South can bid 5♡ confidently.

19

Deal # 2   One More Time

Vul N/S

```
                    ♠ 10 6
                    ♡ K Q 9 5
                    ◊ A K J 10
                    ♣ 5 4 2
♠ J 9 7 5 4 2                        ♠ A K Q 3
♡ 6                                  ♡ J 7 2
◊ Q 9 6 5 2                          ◊ 8 4
♣ 6                                  ♣ Q 10 9 8
                    ♠ 8
                    ♡ A 10 8 4 3
                    ◊ 7 3
                    ♣ A K J 7 3
```

North	East	South	West
1◊	Dbl	Redbl	4♠
Dbl	All	Pass	

East-West went down one, North-South +100. As South can make 6♡ with a successful club finesse, or at least bid 5♡, someone is to blame. Who?

Should South pull North's double? Unclear! 'Right' if North has four hearts or clubs, but 'wrong' if East has those suits as his takeout double promised.

As usual, the blame falls on South for his initial redouble. A better auction:

North	East	South	West
1◊	Dbl	1♡	4♠
5♡	All	Pass	

With only 3 HCP but six spades and great shape, West realizes that North and South likely have a game somewhere, so he makes it hard for them to find their own best contract.

Deal # 3   Defensive Ploys

West	North	East	South
P	P	P	1♣
Dbl	Redbl	?	

Not vul against vul, you, East, hold ♠ Q10987 ♡ QJ7 ◊ 8 ♣ 10953. Would you have opened 1♠, or a Weak 2♠, at favorable vulnerability in third seat?

We hope not. Psyching 1♠ or 2♠ might work but can prove disastrous if partner believes you. Worse, next time you open in third seat with genuine values, your partner may fear you've psyched again and may fail to put you in a cold game.

So you pass and your passed partner makes a takeout double, redoubled by North. Now what? Are you passing again?

We hope not. As partner has shown both majors, you can jump to 2♠ ... or better still, 3♠.

```
                    ♠ 4
                    ♡ K 9 5 4 2
                    ◊ A J 10 7 3
                    ♣ Q 7
    ♠ K J 6 3                        ♠ Q 10 9 8 7
    ♡ A 8 6 3                        ♡ Q J 7
    ◊ K 9 6                          ◊ 8
    ♣ 8 2                            ♣ 10 9 5 3
                    ♠ A 5 2
                    ♡ 10
                    ◊ Q 5 4 2
                    ♣ A K J 6 4
```

With the ◊K on side, North-South can make 3NT, but they can also make 6◊. Do you think they will find their way to either contract if you jump to 3♠?

North should have bid 1♡ while he still had the chance and might have reached 5◊, making six. Note that East can take seven tricks in 4♠ doubled for -500, saving 3 IMPs or a bundle of matchpoints, as North-South can score 600 or 620 in a vulnerable game.

CHAPTER

FOUR

A SIDE NOTE

A SIDE NOTE

Before discussing redoubles further, we must distinguish between two radically different kinds of doubles There are doubles by your left-hand opponent that come round to you, and doubles by your right-hand opponent.

As *cultural* meanings of many doubles have replaced their natural meanings, so also cultural meanings of redoubles have replaced their natural meanings. The most common doubles are of opening suit bids, and the most common redoubles are responder's redoubles thereof.

In current bridge culture and in most bridge teaching, responder's redouble of an opening suit bid is defined as showing high-card strength, an *Oomph* Redouble: *any hand with 10 or more high-card points* ("HCP").

Some books and teachers tout this Oomph Redouble as the *only* acceptable call for a hand that meets that point-count threshold. Often that's the end of the story. But other teachers and writers are careful to make an exception for hands with *primary* support for opener's suit.

'Primary support' is not exactly the same as a fit. Three to an ace, king or queen provides a fit for partner's suit, but you should think of *primary support* as a holding with which you'd gladly *jump-raise* partner. This varies with the rank of the suit. For a major, four-card support will suffice, but for a minor, five-card support is needed. Why?

Because you want to be confident of *at least an 8-card fit.* Yes, partner's 1♡ opening normally delivers at least five hearts, and his 1♣ opening normally delivers at least four clubs. But sometimes, even if no more that 10% of the time, partner will have perfectly good reasons for opening one card short. Secondary support can wait when responder has the normal 10 or more high-card points, but primary support mustn't wait to support.

To show primary support for opener's major with at least 10 HCP, responder must use a convention. The one commonly available is 'Jordan,' which promises at least 10 HCP. The American player Robert Jordan may have invented it independently, but the British expert Alan Truscott, who emigrated to America in 1964 to become the bridge columnist for the *New York Times*, claims to have invented it first.

Many decades later, Danny invented an adjunct to Jordan that limits it to limit raise values. With a full-fledged game force, responder can use *Kinneret*, an artificial double-jump to 3NT instead.

To show primary support for opener's minor, responder may use Jordan, but in order to let opener become notrump declarer, many expert pairs use *Criss-Cross,* a jump-shift in the other minor for their strong minor-suit raises.

Criss-Cross comes at a price, the loss of the natural jump shift in the other minor This brings us to another exception to 'always redouble with 10 HCP or more.' Responder's jump shift, when played as natural and invitational, is a treatment with some merit. We're unsure whether this price for Criss-Cross is too high, but we are sure that any of these conventional raises is better than none.

Here's a new idea: *Two-Way Inverted Truscott* ('TWIT'), yet another application of the transfer principle. After a double of a 1♣ or 1♦ opening, responder's single jump raise is a limit raise while 2NT does double duty.

It is either an artificial weak preemptive raise *or* a game-forcing raise, just like other transfer bids often are. Opener learns of responder's strength when responder then rebids voluntarily beyond three of the agreed minor.

Redoubles by the opening bidder over Righty's balancing doubles have a default meaning: strong balanced hand. With a strong unbalanced hand, opener *bids*.

Natural "business" redoubles are less useful than business doubles, especially at duplicate bridge. We have other names for 'business' redoubles. With apologies to Gordon Gekko, we'll affirm "Greed is good." Well, sometimes---but not often. But in the absence of a clear understanding, Greedy Redoubles are the default.

Lefty and Pancho

Danny calls them Lefty and Pancho, but we'll call them Lefty and Righty here. Your problems and opportunities vary according to which of them doubles you.

When Lefty doubles, you have a chance to end the auction by passing. If the bid doubled was artificial, you'll seldom want to pass, though we can cite auctions where you might.

Suppose partner opens 2NT and you hold ♠ 4 ♡ 109862 ◊ QJ1097 ♣ 72. You respond 3◊, which you play as a Jacoby Transfer, intending to pass his 3♡ or play in 4♡ if opener super-accepts. If Lefty's lead-directing double comes round to you, we trust you'll pass cheerfully.

But now suppose you have ♠ 4 ♡ 109862 ◊ 72 ♣ QJ1097. This time you'd better not pass Lefty's double of your Jacoby Transfer. Now you have two choices:
3♡ and redouble. 3♡ will get you to 3♡ from your side. Should you redouble to get partner to bid 3♡?

Some say yes---that a redouble restates the message you sent with the bid that got doubled---and that here a redouble would be a retransfer. There danger lurks: a possible -1000 if partner forgets---or if it's you who have forgotten, and you never made an agreement with your present partner to play re-transfer redoubles.

Here's a general principle to guide you: *Don't tell the same story twice.*

So when Lefty doubles your *artificial* bid, your redouble must tell a new story. In this case, you'd better have diamonds. Does that mean you *should* redouble with ◊ QJ1097?

Even though a greedy redouble is available, you should refrain from making one. Making 3◊ doubled will get you a bushel of IMPs or a near-top at matchpoints. No need to *gild the lily.*

Redoubling incurs two risks. The first is that you may scare the opponents away. Are you prepared to double them in 3♠, and will that earn you a better score than you expect in 3◊ doubled?

The second is that you may confuse your partner. *You* may not have agreed to play re-transfer redoubles, but he may play them with another partner. Will you blame him if *he* runs to 3♡? Like many other modern conventions, re-transfer redoubles can bite you. More on this in a later chapter.

Things are different when Lefty doubles your side's bid for takeout and Righty passes for penalties. For example, with ♠ K1053 ♡ Q974 ◊ A96 ♣ A5, you might open 1◊. We would, but we'd be terribly scared if Lefty's takeout double were to be passed around to us. Now our redouble, sometimes called an 'SOS' redouble, begs partner to run to *some other suit*.

Likewise, if you pass partner's suit opening, and Righty makes a penalty pass of Lefty's balancing double, your redouble can only be SOS.

But do not think that all redoubles of Lefty's doubles are SOS. 'SOS' applies only to *vague* natural bids. When the opening is a Weak Two-Bid, for example, and Righty makes a penalty pass of Lefty's takeout double, the Weak Two-Bidder can't have enough in the unbid suits to offer or make a choice among them. His only choice is to tough it out. Low honors like jacks and tens, high spot-cards like nines and eights in the suit will help. Again, more on this in the chapter on SOS redoubles.

Things are different when Righty doubles your partner's bid. Now your pass doesn't end the auction---and constitutes another option when otherwise his bid would be forcing. The natural meaning of your pass is "I have nothing to say *at this turn*," but it can be assigned artificial meanings.

Moreover, you have a redouble available to send a message you otherwise couldn't. The natural meaning of a redouble is, of course, "I like it!"---greed. But when Righty's double is not a penalty double as it seldom is in modern bridge, Greedy Redoubles are useless. So the cultural meaning of this redouble is *high-card strength*, and other artificial meanings are possible.

CHAPTER FIVE

ADVANCER'S CALLS AFTER RESPONDER REDOUBLES DEALS 4 – 7

Here is a common auction: 1◇ - Dbl – Redbl – 1♡. Two simple questions:
(1) How many hearts and how many HCP does the 1♡ bid show?
(2) Does this 'free bid' promise values, length, or both?

Let's think about what's going on here. First, partner's takeout double says "I hope we can make a contract in an unbid suit, and I'd like you to help choose which one." Another way of putting it: a takeout double is a simultaneous overcall in the two or three unbid suits.

After Righty redoubles, we know that most likely the deal does not belong to our side. So now our main tasks are first to escape or minimize the damage that our opponents might inflict on us, and second to impede their bidding when we have suits and shape enough to do so.

We can't do this by passing to show weakness, but we can by bidding our suits if we have any real preferences among them. Advances that might imply strength in the absence of the redouble now show shape. The doubler must assume that our bids are obstructive, not constructive.

As partner of the takeout doubler of 1◇, you hold:
  ♠ 43 ♡ 97532 ◇ 964 ♣ 864. What is your side's best contract?

Almost surely 1♡, even if they double. You shouldn't want to have to reach 2♡. But that's what you'll likely reach if you pass on the misguided theory that 1♡ is a 'free bid' showing positive values, e.g., a similar hand with the kings instead of the threes in the majors. What do you think will happen if you pass, viewing 1♡ as a 'free bid' that shows at least 6 HCP?

Partner has ♠ AJ105 ♡ KJ6 ◇ 105 ♣ KQ32 and will bid 1♠. Righty doubles. Many large penalties come against doubled one-and two-level contracts without fits, few against high-level contracts with both high cards and fits. Here we are in 1♠ doubled.

Partner	You
♠ AJ105	♠ 43
♡ KJ6	♡ 97532
◇ 105	◇ 964
♣ KQ32	♣ 864

In 1♠ doubled, partner would get one club and two spade tricks: down four. Of course, we'd run to 2♡. But why run to two hearts when you could have walked to one heart?

So much for the myth that 'free bids' show values over the redouble. We view them as *pressure bids*. Failure to make them can be very expensive indeed. Someone has to bid 1♡ and that someone is you, the partner with five hearts, not the partner with three.

What does a pass over the redouble mean? Its natural meaning is "Nothing to say at this time." Here it says also, "You pick the suit, Pard, I can stand whichever suit you choose, or run safely if I don't like your choice."

We'd bid 1♡ with a 2=4=4=3 yarborough, as we couldn't stand partner to run to 1♠. But we'd pass with a 3=4=3=3 hand, even with queens in all three unbid suits, expecting partner to bid four-card suits up the line.

Another important reason for bidding:

1♡ Dbl Redbl ? What do you call with ♠ 64 ♡ 75432 ◊ 86 ♣ J853?

Run to 2♣. If you pass, partner will likely bid 1♠ and get doubled. You'll have to run to 2♣ anyhow. Once the opponents start doubling, they are in a doubling mode and they will probably double any rescue.

Your best shot to avoid doubles is to bid promptly and confidently.

					Donkey Hands			
1♡	Dbl	Redbl	?	(a)	♠ J54	♡ 987	◊ 108643	♣ 93
				(b)	♠ 54	♡ 987	◊ 108643	♣ J93

Remember the donkey who starved to death because he was equidistant between equally scrumptious bales of hay and couldn't decide which way to turn? That's us as we try to decide between two theories.

Bale of Hay Number One: pass and let partner rescue himself. He may escape undoubled in spades or clubs, but if they double, we can bid 2◊ later to rescue him.

Bale of Hay Number Two: bid 2◊ now. If we pass first and let them start doubling partner in 1♠ or 2♣, they'll never stop. So don't let them start.

More Donkey Hands?

1♡	Dbl	Redbl ?	(c) ♠ J54	♡ 987	◊ 93	♣ 108643	
			(d) ♠ 54	♡ 987	◊ J93	♣ 108643	
			(e) ♠ 54	♡ 987	◊ J943	♣ 10863	

(c) is *not* a Donkey Hand. Passing is not an option. If you pass, partner may well pull to 2◊ with five diamonds. Now you *can't* run to 2♣.

(d) is *not* a Donkey Hand. If you pass, you won't mind playing in diamonds when partner runs to 2◊ with five, but you'll be in trouble when he runs to 1♠, for now a 2♣ rescue will *offer a choice of minors*.

(e) is *not* a Donkey Hand.

Bale of Hay Number Two is looking tastier and tastier, for it can be boiled down to: *With a clear choice among the unbid suits, make it now.*

Direct and *Delayed* differ. *Direct* shows a clear choice. *Delayed* implies tolerance for some other choice.

To make things clearer, we must set aside the distinctions between majors and minors, and between higher-ranking and lower-ranking suits.

Instead, think of one of the three subway systems of New York City, the BMT. The initials stand for 'Bottom,' 'Middle,' and 'Top' unbid suits.

In this case the rank of the unbid suits is *spades – clubs – diamonds.* from bottom to top, and the competing theories apply only when advancer's clear preference is for T, the top suit, *diamonds*.

Had the redoubled opening been 1◊, *clubs* would have been the top suit T. If advancer's only four- or five-card suit is B or M, he *must* bid it now.

1♠ Dbl Redbl ?   You hold ♠ Q542 ♡ J72 ◇ J42 ♣ J92

Pass to deny a preference among the unbid suits. Don't bid a natural 1NT, which would be constructive, showing a balanced 8-10 HCP, had Righty passed. But not when he redoubles, as you can't expect to have such a hand. There aren't enough high cards in the deck.

As of now, there's no such bid as a natural 1NT after responder redoubles. But if you bear with us for a while, we'll show you how you *can* use 1NT.

As responder's redouble marks you with less than the minimum strength needed for a constructive advance of partner's takeout double, a jump is obstructive, not constructive.

With ♠ QJ10753 ♡ 53 ◇ 98 ♣ 643 or similar, jump in spades to show length, not strength, over a redouble of any other suit.

RUN, BABY, RUN!

Rule: After your partner doubles an opposing suit opening and responder redoubles, you and your partner must never play in a redoubled contract. If either of you redoubles, the other must run.

In the examples that follow, the auction has begun 1♠ – Dbl – Redbl – ?

With ♠ 8642 ♡ 6 ◇ J974 ♣ 10753, just pass, letting partner run to the cheapest suit in which he has four or five cards. (Option - See Scrambling 1NT in Chapter 15)

With ♠ 8642 ♡ J974 ◇ 10753 ♣ 6, you can pass also. If partner runs to 2♣, your 2◇ rebid next will offer a choice of red suits. But if your RHO doubles 2♣, you can redouble, letting your partner, the stronger hand declare.

With ♠ 8642 ♡ J974 ◇ 6 ♣ 10753, you can pass the redouble too. If partner runs to 2◇ and responder passes, you can correct to 2♡, but if responder doubles as he usually will, you can do better still by redoubling to require partner to run to 2♡. Which brings us to a radical new idea.

STERNBERG TRANSFERS

Why not strive to have the stronger hand, the takeout doubler, declare? If you and your partner adopt Sternberg Transfers, you can often do so.

Once we observe that a 1NT advance is never natural after the redouble, let's define 1NT and all two-bids in lower-ranking suits as *transfers to the next suit up*, except of course transfers to opener's suit.

Two of a *higher-ranking suit* is weak.

Over 1♠ redoubled, 1NT shows clubs, 2♣ shows diamonds, 2◊ shows hearts.

Over 1♡ redoubled, 1♠ is natural, 1NT shows clubs, 2♣ shows diamonds, 2♠ is weak.

Over 1◊ redoubled, 1♡ and 1♠ are natural, 1NT shows clubs, 2♡ and 2♠ are weak.

Over 1♣ redoubled, 1◊, 1♡ and 1♠ are natural. 2◊, 2♡ and 2♠ are weak.

Now the Donkey bids 1♡-double-redouble-2♣ "Alert: diamonds!".

With a better hand and suit, e.g. ♠ 54 ♡ 987 ◊ KQ1083 ♣ J93, advancer can raise the doubler's 2◊ 'acceptance' to 3◊. He will often get the chance, as responder will usually pass 2◊ in hope that opener can double.

32

DANNY'S DUETS

Sternberg Transfers handle advancer's hands with one possible trump suit, and pass-then-redouble or pass-then-run can handle advancer's hands with two possible trump suits. Can we bid hands with two unbid *five-card* equally well?

Yes, if we're willing to increase the level, as we usually should with 5-5 in two unbid suits.

Danny's Duets use the 'Unusual 2NT' to show the two lowest unbid suits, and the Michaels Cue Bid to show the two highest unbid suits. Easy to remember?

What's left? The 'transfer' into opener's suit shows the Top and Bottom Unbid Suits ('TABUS').

1♣-Dbl-Redbl-1NT = ◊+♠   1◊-Dbl-Redbl-2♣ = ♣+♠
1♡-Dbl-Redbl-2◊ = ♠+♣   1♠-Dbl-Redbl-2♡ = ♡+♣

Sternberg Transfers and Danny's Duets must be alerted, of course.

Deal # 4　　After RHO's Redouble

As South you hold: ♠ 7643 ♡ 1032 ◊ 10852 ♣ Q6

West	North	East	South
1♡	Dbl	Redbl	?

You have a terrible hand and you pass. The auction continues:

West	North	East	South
1♡	Dbl	Redbl	P
P	2♣	Dbl	?

Well, that's not good. Partner's double showed at least three spades so you run to 2♠. 2♠ doubled becomes the final contract. Could you have done better?

Yes, you could have been in 1♠, perhaps doubled, perhaps not. But by passing, you left partner to rescue himself and he bid his five-card suit.

```
              ♠ A J 10
              ♡ A J
              ◊ A 9 3
              ♣ J 7 5 4 3
  ♠ K 9 5                    ♠ Q 8 2
  ♡ K Q 7 6 4                ♡ 9 8 5
  ◊ K Q 4                    ◊ J 7 6
  ♣ 10 2                     ♣ A K 9 8
              ♠ 7 6 4 3
              ♡ 10 3 2
              ◊ 10 8 5 2
              ♣ Q 6
```

If South had bid 1♠, neither opponent can comfortably double 1♠ and East will bid 2♡. By bidding 1♠, South can get his side out of trouble and East-West would have ended in a part score. 2♣ doubled would have gone down two or three.

South	West	North	East
1◊	Dbl	Redbl	?

East holds ♠ J97432 ♡ 4 ◊ Q10764 ♣ 3   What should he bid?

Lots of spades! Not 1♠ or 2♠, but 3♠, or perhaps 4♠ on favorable vulnerability. That should shut them out! This jump is weak. There aren't nearly enough high cards in the deck for all four hands to be strong, as there are only 40 HCP in the deck.

Except of course in the deck that some of P. Hal Sims' friends rigged for him in the 1930s. That one contained 42 HCP, as they gave both defenders a ♠Q to challenge his queen-guessing prowess.

On the auction, East can't have more than 7 HCP.

Let North and South guess what to do at the four- or five-level. Now it's their problem, not yours. They'll often guess wrong. Before you sprain your shoulder patting yourself on the back, remember your bold preempt wouldn't have created this mess for the opponents if not for North's misguided redouble.

```
                    ♠ 5
                    ♡ K Q 6 5 2
                    ◊ K 5 3
                    ♣ K J 10 7
    ♠ K Q 8 6                       ♠ J 9 7 4 3 2
    ♡ J 8 3                         ♡ 4
    ◊ 9                             ◊ Q 10 7 6 4
    ♣ A Q 8 6 4                     ♣ 3
                    ♠ A 10
                    ♡ A 10 9 7
                    ◊ A J 8 2
                    ♣ 9 5 2
```

North should bid 1♡ after the takeout double instead of redoubling. Now he is still sitting there trying to guess what to do.

Let's just leave him guessing and go on to the next deal.

Deal # 6　　　Getting In There

South	West	North	East
1♠	Dbl	Redbl	?

East holds ♠ 743　♡ 103　◊ KQ1094　♣ 964.　　Should he bid or pass?

East should bid 3◊, which is a weak preempt, not an invitation to game. Again, how much high-card strength can East have? Actually, he has a maximum on the auction. It's important to bid for two reasons.

Sure as shooting, North and South have a spade fit. Unless West continues the preempt in diamonds, he'll be on lead against a spade contract. Any lead but a diamond may blow a trick, and any chance to beat the contract.

```
              ♠ A K 10
              ♡ J 9 8 6 5
              ◊ 5 3
              ♣ J 10 2
  ♠ 6 2                      ♠ 7 4 3
  ♡ A Q 7 2                  ♡ 10 3
  ◊ J 7 6 2                  ◊ K Q 10 9 4
  ♣ A Q 8                    ♣ 9 6 4
              ♠ Q J 9 8 5
              ♡ K 4
              ◊ A 8
              ♣ K 7 5 3
```

The auction will continue:

South	West	North	East
1♠	Dbl	Redbl	3◊
P	P	3♠	All Pass

Looks like down one on the diamond lead that West might well have found in any event. Could North and South have avoided this unfortunate result? Perhaps, had North bid 2♠ instead of redoubling.

Deal # 7   When Enough is Enough

Vul Both

♠ 9 8 5 2	West	North	East	South
♡ 10 7 3	…	…	1♡	Dbl
◊ 9 4	Redbl	1♠	P	?
♣ J 9 8 4				

♠ K 10 3
♡ A 6 5
◊ Q J 7 5 3
♣ 6 5

♠ A 7 6
♡ Q J 9 4 2
◊ 10 6
♣ K Q 10

♠ Q J 4
♡ K 8
◊ A K 8 2
♣ A 7 3 2

What should South have done over East's 1♡ opening? Double or overcall 1NT? With support for all unbid suits and the wrong kind of heart stopper, we much prefer doubling. With ♡K8, he can't even hold up once.

So South doubles. West redoubles. Probably a good thing that South did not bid 1NT as West would surely double. North bids 1♠.

How many spades and how many HCP is North showing? When East passes, should South act again?

To even ask this question is to overbid. North rates to be broke. He is bidding because he can't stand for South to run to diamonds.

Good players know when to quit. Yes, you have 17 HCP but few tricks. You have only three spades. You will surely be doubled in 2♠. Even if not doubled, 2♠ is likely to go down two for -200. The auction continues:

East	South	West	North
1♡	Dbl	Redbl	1♠
P	P	2♡	All Pass

West bids 2♡, indicating a three-card limit raise and everyone passes.

Did you dodge the bullet?

For more on 1NT overcalls, see Danny's brief discussion on the next page.

Time Out for Danny's *Obiter Dictum*

In the 20th century, natural 1NT overcalls probably broke even. They produced some good scores for bidding and making part-scores and some bad scores for going down. They led to a few games that made and somewhat more often, they led to disasters from responders' bruising penalty doubles.

But who plays to win? Most play for the joy of bidding notrumps and declaring contracts. A modest net loss from making natural 1NT overcalls is not too steep a price to pay.

By the 21st century, however, players started overcalling 1NT with the wrong hands, e.g., with three low cards or a doubleton king in opener's suit.

By then too, many had been taught that 'front of the card' applied, not realizing that it was advantageous to put the 1♥ opener, rather than his weak partner, on opening lead. Worse still, 'system on' left no way to get out in two of a minor.

2♣ served as Stayman for spades only in this case and 2◊ was a silly transfer to opener's presumed five-card heart suit.

Worst of all after either standard advances, cue bid only force or systems on, none of my partners ever remembered on which method they'd agreed---not even when I caved and said, "All right, I'll play the idiotic 'front of card.'"

Expecting a 50% failure rate, I experienced a 100% failure rate. Impossible to explain? Hint: what if instead of memory, my partners relied on 'mind-reading,' i.e. tempo and other mannerisms? Not today, thank you, nor ever for me.

Better never to overcall 1NT than to make natural 1NT overcalls! But better still to use 1NT overcalls artificially, for two-suiters to fill a gap. Use 2NT for two lowest, Michaels Cue Bid for two highest, and 1NT for Top and Bottom Unbid Suits, similar to Danny's Duets after one-of-a-suit – Dbl – Redbl.

CHAPTER SIX

OPENER'S REBID

WHEN RESPONDER

REDOUBLES

DEAL 8

First, here are some rules that we urge upon you. Your partner will not be happy if you violate and pass a forcing bid, saying "I opened light." Why would you ever 'open light' anyway?

Rule 1: The redouble sets up a forcing situation. To what level? At least to 2NT or three of opener's suit. Normally, you'll either declare the contract or double the opponents.

Some authorities say you *must* outbid your opponents or double them, a theory sometimes expressed as 'Buy it or belt it!'---by which they mean after the redouble, *never* to pass out an opposing bid undoubled.

We disagree. It's much easier to gauge your own side's prospects than the opponents'. You and your partner may know that you have nine hearts between you, including the ♡A and ♡K. But you don't know whether you have two, one or no heart tricks on defense against spades. As far as you can tell, the missing hearts may split 2-2, 3-1 or 4-0. So sometimes you'd do well to sell out to an opposing 3♠ without doubling, settling for -140 or +50 instead of doubling and hoping for +100 while risking -530.

Rule 2: All subsequent doubles by either partner are for penalties.

Rule 3: Doubling the opponents in one of a suit requires at least four decent trumps, including a stopper in case partner wants to bid notrumps.

Rule 4: Passing an opposing runout to one of a suit denies the ability to double it but shows at least two cards in the suit and a willingness to sit if partner doubles.

Let's consider some of your problems as opener after:

You	Lefty	Partner	Righty
1 of a suit	Dbl	Redbl	Pass

What are your options? When should you pass? If you bid, what do your bids mean? Should you describe your hand or stay out of partner's way?

Let's suppose that you opened 1♡. Start by assuming partner has fewer than three hearts and may want to double the runout for penalties. If he has three hearts, he'll have a game-invitational hand or better and he'll bid hearts next, but that's a seldom thing.

Next you need to consider how suitable your hand is for defense. Will you be pleased to sit for partner's likely penalty double?

With a few exceptions that we'll discuss, it's best to pass and let Lefty rescue himself. This tells partner that you are willing to defend if he doubles.

When Lefty runs, partner will clarify his redouble. If he doubles, he expects you will sit for it, as your pass already suggested you would.

If instead you bid before Lefty can rescue himself, you show an unbalanced hand.

You must not bid 1NT to show a balanced minimum. That's what partner will assume you have if you pass.

Does that mean you should *never* rebid 1NT? No. We hate to let a bid lie fallow. So we suggest using 1NT to show an otherwise troublesome hand type that we'll call a *Mini-Reverse One Notrump.*

Each of the hands below is a 5-4-3-1 hand with a singleton in Righty's suit, so you'd like to bid before Lefty can raise to two and give your partner a headache.

The trouble is if you bid your four-card suit now you'd have to bid it at the two-level and force partner to show a preference at the three-level, a rebid called a 'reverse' that requires a very good hand.

Replace the deuce in each of the hands below with the ace of its suit, you'd have ample values to reverse, but with the actual hands, you don't.

Here's where we can put that otherwise idle 1NT rebid to good use.

You	Lefty	Partner	Righty
1♣	Dbl	Redbl	1♠
?			

(a) ♠ 6 ♡ K842 ◊ QJ9 ♣ AK853
    1NT (Alert! One spade, four hearts.)

You	Lefty	Partner	Righty
1◊	Dbl	Redbl	1♠
?			

(b) ♠ 6 ♡ K842 ◊ AK853 ♣ QJ9
    1NT (Alert! One spade, four hearts.)

You	Lefty	Partner	Righty
1♣	Dbl	Redbl	1♡
?			

(c) ♠ QJ9 ♡ 6 ◊ K842 ♣ AK853
    1NT (Alert! One heart, four diamonds.)

You	Lefty	Partner	Righty
1♣	Dbl	Redbl	1♠	(d) ♠ 6 ♡ QJ9 ◊ K842 ♣ AK853
?			Pass

At first, we thought (d) fell under the umbrella of a Mini-Reverse too, but that renders the 1NT rebid ambiguous, and the doubler's possible 2♠ raise may pose an impossible problem for responder.

It's much better to handle one pattern (1=4=3=5) well than two patterns (1=4=3=5 and 1=3=4=5) poorly, and much more useful to find a heart fit than a diamond fit.

Besides, with some 1=3=4=5 hands, e.g. (e) ♠ 6 ♡ QJ9 ◊ AK84 ♣ K8532, we might on rare occasions open 1◊, not 1♣.

Some authorities say any bid, even a jump, denies as much as 15 HCP, so that with strong distributional hands, opener must pass first, then pull responder's anticipated double.

Not always. Responder won't always double the runout. Sometimes he'll bid or pass and then you'll have no double to pull. How will you show your shape then?

May we remind you of Silkwood's Law? If you're short in a suit that an opponent has bid or may bid now, don't wait to bid again later. Rebid the long suit you opened now, or your second suit if you have one, with a jump when sufficiently strong.

You can't rely on 'pass then pull' to distinguish minimum openings from strong ones. By the time you pull, the auction may be awkwardly high, especially if you intended to pull with a jump.

Before discussing your problems when your RHO bids ahead of you, let's look at some examples when he passes.

After 1♠ - Dbl – Redbl – Pass, should you bid or pass?

♠ AQ9642 ♡ 75 ◇ KQJ ♣ 94.	Bid 2♠. You have extra length and only one defensive trick outside.
♠ AKQJ42 ♡ 642 ◇ void ♣ KJ74.	Bid 3♠, You want to declare, not defend despite having a stronger hand.
♠ AK642 ♡ 86 ◇ J2 ♣ A1075.	Pass. With a minimum opening and a semi-balanced hand, you'll be happy to defend, and hope to double 2♣.
♠ KQ7543 ♡ 5 ◇ AQ1064 ♣ 6.	Bid 2◇. You have great playing strength. Start showing your shape *now*.
♠ AKJ1098 ♡ KQ4 ◇ 3 ♣ A98.	Bid 3♠. Or your next turn may come over an opponent's 4◇ and you'll have to bid 5♠ to jump.

Now let's suppose that your RHO bids over the redouble. Most of the principles discussed above apply. Moreover, you may be able to double.

Suppose you hold ♠ AJ ♡ Q1054 ◇ AJ10642 ♣ 5

You	Lefty	Partner	Righty	
1◇	Dbl	Redbl	2♣	Bid 2◇, as you wouldn't sit for partner's possible double.
1◇	Dbl	Redbl	1♡	Double. This shows hearts, not necessarily extra strength. Partner will sit unless he is short in hearts.

Of course, vulnerability matters. Both partners should lean towards bidding games when vulnerable and collecting penalties when the opponents are vulnerable.

Sometimes you may pass and after the doubler rescues himself, partner will pass the buck back to you. This may make life difficult. For example:

Vul against not, you hold ♠ Q642 ♡ 43 ◊ AJ10 ♣ KQJ5

You	Lefty	Partner	Righty
1♣	Dbl	Redbl	1♡
P	2♡	P	P
?			

Partner's failure to double 2♡ marks the opponents with eight or nine hearts. You may want to pass but you mustn't do so below the three-level. His pass is forcing. Bid 2♠ and hope for the best. Partner will play you for something like the hand you have and will have a pretty good idea what to do.

Deal # 8 Opener Bids in Front of the Doubler

N/S Vul

```
              ♠ Q 10 5 2
              ♡ J 6
              ◇ A Q J 4 2
              ♣ A 7
♠ A J 8 4                      ♠ K 9 7 6 3
♡ K 10 2                       ♡ 8 5 3
◇ 8 7 5                        ◇ 10 9 6
♣ K Q 5                        ♣ 9 2
              ♠ void
              ♡ A Q 9 7 4
              ◇ K 3
              ♣ J 10 8 6 4 3
```

In a team event, both Souths opened 1♡, planning to rebid in clubs. Both Wests doubled improperly, perhaps because they play Woodrow Wilson doubles that show '14 points' without appropriate shape.

Edgar Kaplan debunked them in his 1965 classic book *Competitive Bidding in Modern Bridge*, but some players still make them because they don't know how to spell *shmoints*. Over North's anchor redouble, both Easts jumped to 2♠, a weak preempt for obstructive purposes.

What should South do?

Both Souths, being unwilling to sit for a double of 2♠, bid 3♣. They were telling their story while it could be told at a reasonably low level.

At one table, ignoring both South's cry of spade shortness and an auction that suggested everybody had minimal high-card strength, North bid 3NT. A low spade to West's ♠A and West's thoughtful ♠8 return let East preserve the ♠K, his lone entry. When West won the ♡K, the defenders took three more spade tricks to beat 3NT.

At the other table, North took warning from South's 3♣ bid and didn't rush to bid 3NT. Instead, he bid a patient 3◇, then took a mild preference to 4♡ over South's 4♣. With the friendly 3-3 heart break, declarer had ten tricks.

CHAPTER

SEVEN

RESPONDER'S

REBID OPTIONS

DEALS 9 - 10

Let's look a bit deeper into the four options previously mentioned.

(1) A double is a pure penalty double. When you redouble, opener will usually pass at his next turn to see why you redoubled. If he were unwilling to sit for a penalty double, he would have bid at his second turn. A low-level penalty double, even at the 1-level, is one of the most underrated calls in bridge, often leading to big gains. You don't need a big trump stack, just the balance of power, some stuff in the opponent's suit and not too much in partner's suit.

In a problem posed to an expert panel in the ACBL Bulletin (June 2003), you held ♠ 10743 ♡ 3 ◊ AJ84 ♣ AQ86. The auction started:

Partner	RHO	You	LHO
1♡	Dbl	Redbl	P
P	1♠	?	

Thirteen of 14 panelists doubled, despite weak trumps. Experts love to penalize one-level bids. The lone dissenter wanted ♠ Q1043 to double.

What are the ideal features for low-level penalty doubles?

First is a poor fit with partner. Danny's Doubling Guideline says that you should not contemplate a penalty double below the level equal to your length in partner's suit.

Second is length and strength in the opponents' trump suit.

Third is high cards, especially behind the doubler. Vulnerability matters too. If you think you have a vulnerable game, and thus can score +600 or more, a double must earn you +800. If you're not vul and can only score +400 or more in your own game, +500 will be enough.

Opener's pass also encourages doubling, as it suggests that he'll sit. With a singleton or void, he'd have bid in front of you. So his pass shows at least two cards in the suit you're thinking of doubling, and thus a willingness to defend.

How many trumps must you have to double? Normally four, but occasionally three good trumps will do. Remember that your decision depends also on the level of the bid and your length in partner's suit. Do not abandon a chance for a juicy penalty double too readily, especially on favorable vulnerability.

After 1♣ - Dbl, you'd redouble with (a) ♠ AQ42 ♡ QJ86 ◊ J753 ♣ 3 or (b) ♠ KQ42 ♡ AJ ◊ Q652 ♣ 864.

With (a), you plan to double any runout.

With (b), you plan to double 1♠, 1NT or 2◊, but you'll pass 1♡. Opener will know to double 1♡ if he has four hearts. Else he'll make his normal rebid, e.g., 1♠ with four spades.

(2) A delayed raise of opener's suit shows a hand too strong for a direct raise to two *while denying primary support*. A non-jump raise shows a three-card limit raise of opener's major-suit opening but a four-card invitational raise of opener's minor-suit opening.

As it's a raise, responder must count *support*, not high-card points. A reasonable threshold is 11 or a gilt-edged 10 points. Or as many of us do, you might just look at your hand and deem it too strong for a direct raise to two.

Having started with a redouble, you need not jump to then show a three-card limit raise. A redouble followed by a jump shows a three-card *forcing* raise of opener's major. With four-card support, you'd have bid a 'Jordan' 2NT.

Likewise, with five-card support for opener's minor, you'd have used 'Jordan,' 'TWIT' or 'Criss-Cross', a jump shift in the unbid minor, whichever is available in your partnership methods.

With ♠ J106 ♡ 654 ◊ KJ3 ♣ AQ54 or ♠ Q95 ♡ 9752 ◊ AQJ73 ♣ 6, you would redouble partner's 1♠ opening, planning to bid 2♠ next. With another queen, you would redouble then jump to 3♠.

A line on the ACBL convention card says "Redouble implies no fit."

Does it mean anything more than "Don't redouble with *primary* support"? We don't know, but that's standard practice regardless.

(3) Bidding notrump denies the ability to double for penalties, often for fear that the penalty would be too small, especially when you're vulnerable but your opponents are not.

(4) A pass is verboten when the doubler's runout comes round to the opener. Forcing but permissible and often necessary over the doubler's self-rescue, to give opener a chance to wield the axe.

But this can give opener a real headache. Try very hard to avoid these auctions.

For example:

You	LHO	Partner	RHO	
1♠	Dbl	Redbl	P	Opener: ♠ Q7532 ♡ 75 ♦ AQ5 ♣ AJ7
P	2♡	P	P	
???				

Jim (*Dr J*) says "Take two aspirin and call me in the morning."

Danny (the druggist on the corner) sells *Danny's Headache Powder*, a balancing 2NT that by partnership agreement shows a minimum balanced hand, no stopper required, as a cure for all your sorrows and an end to all distress.

(5) A new suit is natural and forcing for one round.

(6) A cue bid is a general game force, showing a hand that is unsuitable for anything mentioned above.

Look at the migraine responder's redouble then pass can give opener.

You	LHO	Partner	RHO		
1♠	Dbl	Redbl	P	You:	♠ Q7532 ♡ 75 ◊ AQ5 ♣ AJ7
P	2♡	P	P	Responder:	♠ J6 ♥ K83 ♦ KJ104 ♣ KQ95
???					

It's either extra-strength Danny's Headache Powder or "Helllp!"

Deal # 9   A Classic Example

As noted, the vast majority of redoubles show either a desire to penalize or strong raises for opener's suit, three-card for a major or four-card support for opener's minor. Let's look at this example.

```
                    ♠ Q J 8 5
                    ♡ 8 3
                    ♢ K 9 8 3
                    ♣ K Q 8
    ♠ A 10 9 6                         ♠ 7 3
    ♡ 6 5                              ♡ K Q 7 4
    ♢ A J 6                            ♢ 10 7 5 2
    ♣ A 9 7 6                          ♣ 4 3 2
                    ♠ K 4 2
                    ♡ A J 10 9 2
                    ♢ Q 4
                    ♣ J 10 5
```

North	East	South	West
P	P	1♡	Dbl
Redbl	2♢	P	P
Dbl	All	Pass	

North has a classic hand for his redouble. Not wanting the doubling to start over West's possible black-suit self-rescue, East bids 2♢. With a balanced hand, South stays out of North's way, suggesting tolerance for a penalty double.

North springs the trap, everybody sits properly and after South's ♢Q opening lead, East figures to go down two or three in a 4-3 fit.

A much better result for North and South than playing in some part-score.

Deal # 10   Which Door ?

You are North with ♠ 10962 ♡ K104 ◇ J1032 ♣ AQ.

South opens 1♡ and West doubles. What are your choices?
Choose from the following four doors: 2♡, 3♡, 2NT, and redouble.

Behind one door the Lady awaits you. Behind the other three lie Tigers.

2♡ would show single raise values, 6 to a drab 10 HCP. Thanks to your tens,
  you're too strong.

3♡ has two fatal flaws. A jump raise is a weak preempt, and should deliver a fourth
  heart, with shortness somewhere and at most 6 HCP.
  Wrong shape, wrong strength.

2NT is an artificial raise, 'Jordan', that shows invitational or better values which
  you have, but promises four-card or longer support which you do not have.

To keep all three tigers hungry, you must redouble, planning to bid hearts next.
That rebid will show a hand too strong for a single raise but only three trumps.
The auction continues:

South	West	North	East
1♡	Dbl	Redbl	P
P	1♠	?	Now what?

Despite your four spades, you must not even think of doubling. Your fit for
partner's suit, hearts, precludes doubling short of the three-level.
  Bid 2♡, showing limit-raise values. 3♥ would be game-forcing.

South has a minimum. ♠ K8 ♡ QJ985 ◇ K97 ♣ KJ4, and passes 2♡.

Did you miss a game? South will likely lose two spades, one heart and two
diamonds. Aren't you happy to be at the two-level?

CHAPTER

EIGHT

REDOUBLES

AFTER WE

FIND A FIT

DEAL 11

REDOUBLES AFTER FINDING A FIT

After we have found a trump fit, we may either stop in a partscore or seek a game or slam. If one opponent makes a takeout double, what should our redouble mean?

Let's consider four different auctions and see if we can come to some logical conclusions.

(1) | Partner | RHO | You | LHO |
|---|---|---|---|
| 1♡ | P | 2♡ | P |
| P | Dbl | Redbl | |

(2) | Partner | RHO | You | LHO |
|---|---|---|---|
| | | 1♡ | P |
| 2♡ | Dbl | Redbl | |

(3) | Partner | RHO | You | LHO |
|---|---|---|---|
| 1♣ | P | 1♡ | P |
| 2♡ | Dbl | Redbl | |

(4) | Partner | RHO | You | LHO |
|---|---|---|---|
| 1♣ | P | 1♡ | P |
| 2♡ | P | P | Dbl |
| Redbl | | | |

What do these redoubles mean? Extra strength? Extra length? Are we now in a forcing auction?

Unless defined otherwise specifically, these redoubles promise undisclosed extra strength, deny extra length and suggest defending against an opposing runout. With extra shape or length but not extra strength, show your shape by bidding.

In Auctions (1) and (4), where the raiser, a limited hand redoubles, he shows minimal length, here three cards in the suit, but with maximal high-card strength. In (1), responder may have a hand like ♠ KQ5 ♡ 964 ◊ 1095 ♣ A1073 and be eager to defend.

In Auctions (2) and (3), the redoubler is unlimited and shows at least game-try values.

In (2), opener might have ♠ 64 ♡ KQJ53 ◊ AQ4 ♣ AQ10. while typical for (3) would be ♠ KJ8 ♡ AJ86 ◊ Q1063 ♣ 63.

Do not redouble just because you expect the contract to make or to make with an overtrick.

If you merely have extra trump length without extra defense, do not redouble. It will only give the opponents extra room to find a fit. Instead, re-raise immediately.

For example, with ♠ A63 ♡ QJ96 ◊ 76 ♣ 10642 in Auction (3), bid 3♡ immediately. You have one more heart than promised and you're willing to take the push.

With ♠ K ♡ AQ1075 ◊ 108 ♣ AQ753 in Auction (2), make a standard 3♣ game try. Partner will love his hand if he has the filling kings in both your suits. You will love it when he puts his hand on the table as dummy in 4♡.

Remember the mantra that Maharishi Mahesh Daniel gave Danny on his first pilgrimage to the Himalayas: "Balanced Hands Defend." Ah, but a year later the Bagwhan Three Ruffnisht countered with "Suits and Shape Compete." Danny is still trying to figure out which guru to believe. Jim says, "Why not believe both?"

After we've redoubled to show extra strength, all later doubles are for penalty but with a bonus of safety. The doubler's partner has a harbor to which to return with unexpected shortness in the doubled suit or extra length in the raised suit.

Are you in a forcing auction after a redouble in these situations?

If the redoubler is limited, as in Auctions (1) and (4), no. But if the redoubler is unlimited, as in auctions (2) and (3), the raiser can not sell out to the opponents. At this level, 'buy it or belt it' *does* apply.

Deal # 11   The Promiscuous Balancer

```
            ♠ A K 7 6 4        Board-a-Match, both sides vulnerable
            ♡ Q 7              WEST    NORTH   EAST    SOUTH
            ◊ J 8 7 4          …       …       …       P
            ♣ K 8             P       1♠      P       2♣*
♠ 3 2                  ♠ J 10 5    P       2♠**    P       P
♡ J 10 6 3             ♡ A 5 2     ?
◊ Q 10 9              ◊ A 5 2
♣ A 10 9 6           ♣ 5 4 3 2    *Two-Way Reverse Drury
            ♠ Q 9 8            ("three-card limit raise")
            ♡ K 9 8 4
            ◊ K 6 3            **no desire for game
            ♣ Q J 7
```

Doug Drury invented Drury to protect against his partner of the time, Eric Murray, a great player from Canada. His third-seat major openings were sometimes based on hands too weak to show in a book. Originally, it was a passed-hand 2♣ response to 1♡ or 1♠ that asked Eric to reply 2◊ to reveal a psych or semi-psych. Now many pairs use a version in which a passed-hand 2♣ (three card support) and 2◊ (four or more card support) invite game in opener's major, and opener's two-of-his-major rebid rejects game.

Current bridge dogma suggests not to let opponents play at the two-level when they seem to have found a fit. Most balance without hope of making a contract of their own, just to push their opponents one level higher.

In keeping with his religion, West balanced with a takeout double. Having limited his hand, North redoubled to show that his 1♠ opening was not a Murray Special. As we've noted, with extra shape, North might have bid again, but with maximum high-card strength for his 2♠, he redoubled.

East ran to his club miniskirt, but when South doubled 3♣, (after redouble, all subsequent doubles are business doubles), East ran from the club frying pan into the heart fire. South doubled 3♡. Repeated trump leads put East down four, -1100.

West's teammates at the other table reached a skinny 3NT. The splits favored North-South, who chalked up +600. By balancing, the Rumpelstiltskin of the West had spun gold into straw. Had West pushed his opponents to 3♠, he would merely have pushed them where 2♣ said they were willing to go.

CHAPTER

NINE

SOS

REDOUBLES

DEALS 12 - 15

Years ago, Karen Walker wrote that if you ask any bridge player what was the biggest minus score he ever had, he'll likely tell a redouble story, in particular, an SOS redouble tragedy.

Karen retold the 1973 story of expert Ron Smith. When he compared scores with his teammates, instead of hearing the usual "win six", "push", or "lose two", that he expected upon reporting +430 on a routine deal, he heard from his teammate Roger Lord:

"Lose 'em all," meaning "lose 24," the maximum the scoring table permits on any single deal. Roger had played in a 4♣ cuebid, an 'SOS' redouble for rescue but left in. 4♣ redoubled minus 4600 was a 4170-point swing, off the IMP scale that ends with 4000+.

More than a decade earlier, Danny played in a tournament in which a teammate returned and rattled off the score on Board 13. "Plus 2200. They passed an SOS redouble. Plus 2200. We won this board big."

"No, *you* didn't," said Danny. His teammate's grin turned to a frown.

"Oh, Board 13. I knew 13 was an unlucky number," said the teammate.

"*We* won this board, not you," continued Danny. "Plus 2800. They passed a redouble of a four-heart Texas Transfer. Responder meant it as a retransfer. I don't want to hear you call 13 unlucky." That was a 5000-point swing.

Rudolf Kock and Einar Werner of Stockholm, Sweden, leading international players of the 1940s and '50s originated the SOS redouble, originally called *Koch-Werner Redoubles*.

Making a doubled contract at any form of scoring is almost always a good result. If you expect to make a low-level doubled contract, it would be foolish to redouble just to increase the already fine score you can earn by passing and playing the doubled contract. Why give the opponents a chance to run? Why jeopardize a splendid result?

So the redouble of a low-level penalty double can be put to better use: to scream "We gotta get outta this place!" and ask partner where to escape.

A more formal definition of an 'SOS redouble': *After a penalty double of a bid below game, or a penalty pass of a takeout double, a redouble that begs partner to run to another suit.*

How can we recognize an SOS redouble when we see one?
Here are our Redoubling for Rescue Requirements:

RRR1   The doubled suit has not been raised or otherwise agreed.

RRR2   The redoubler can expect his partner to have a suit to which to run, but doesn't know which. He won't have any if he's shown a one-suiter, as by preempting.in his suit or rebidding it voluntarily.

RRR3   The auction is at a reasonably low level.

RRR4   The double was a penalty double, or a takeout double passed for penalties.

RRR5   You can expect a pass to end the auction.

After:	LHO	Partner	RHO	You
	1◊	1♡	P	P
	Dbl	P	P	?

you would do well to redouble with ♠ QJ75 ♥ 2 ◊ 853 ♣ Q10975. Righty's penalty pass portends a bad heart stack and you can hope partner will fare better in 1♠ or 2♣, even if doubled.

59

After: LHO   Partner   RHO   You

LHO	Partner	RHO	You
		2♥*	2♠
Dbl	P	P	?

*Weak Two-Bid

Redouble with ♠ AJ753 ♡ 5 ◊ Q106 ♣ KQJ8. You have run into a spade stack, so urge partner to bid his longer minor.

After:	LHO	Partner	RHO	You
				1♣
	Dbl	P	P	?

Redouble with ♠ AJ96 ♡ K106 ◊ Q74 ♣ A32 to urge partner to run. His duty after your redouble is clear. He must not pass with anything less than ♣ QJ10xx.

LHO	Partner	RHO	You
		1♠	2◊
P	P	Dbl	P
P	Redbl	P	2♡

♠ A107
♡ 853
◊ AKJ864
♣ 5

Partner won't be unhappy to catch you with three low hearts. Thank your lucky stars that you don't have two low hearts and two low clubs!

AVOIDING MISUSE

Although every convention gets misused sometimes, the SOS redouble is near the top of the list. (No convention will ever top Blackwood.) Remember, the doubled bid must be natural and must have been doubled or passed for penalties.

LHO	Partner	RHO	You
1♡	1NT	Dbl	?

♠ 743
♡ 86
◊ J753
♣ 8532

"Oh sinner man, where you gonna run to?"

As you have nowhere to run, pass and let partner take his lumps in 1NT doubled.

1♡	2♣	Dbl^	?

^ Negative Double

♠ J9753
♡ 975
◊ Q10753
♣ Void

A redouble would show a good hand. Pass and hope opener bids.

Often it's best to sit for a double or run to a suit of your own. If partner opens 1♡, you'll pass with ♠ J10753 ♡ void ◊ J765 ♣ 10842.

But if Lefty doubles and Righty passes for penalties, you'll do better to run to 1♠ than make an SOS redouble and risk getting doubled in 2♣ or 2◇ on a 4-3 fit. You keep the auction at the one-level and avoid revealing the panic that an SOS redouble conveys.

The next example poses a thornier problem that involves another variable.

LHO	Partner	RHO	You		♠ J8653
1♡	2♣	P	P		♡ J98
Dbl	P	P	?		◇ A1063
					♣ 3

Does your partner make loosey-goosy two-level overcalls with mediocre hands and five-card suits? If so, then it's "Run, baby, run!"

But a sound bidder waits for a good hand, a good six-bagger and opening or near-opening strength to overcall at the two-level, especially when his partner has yet to call. So *know thy partner.*

You should also take the form of contest into account. A very good player used to be a regular in Danny's rubber-bridge games. The two did well when they cut each other as partners. Then after the last rubber-bridge club in Los Angeles folded, they played matchpoints at a local duplicate bridge club.

Oops, it was all too often, "I'm surprised at you. Good old reliable Danny! How could you overcall with such trash?"

Lead-directing overcalls on trash are a losing proposition at rubber bridge or IMPs. Yes, sometimes they save a trick and help you beat the contract, but more often the trick they save is only a 20- or 30-point overtrick. But at matchpoints or Board-a-Match that 20- or 30-point overtrick can make a significant difference.

Some of Danny's non-vulnerable overcalls at matchpoints are hairy. He claims he could average 70% if the rules let him double his own overcalls for penalties. So if you were to partner one of us at matchpoints, you might scream 'SOS' opposite Danny but Jim is more solid. You can let him stew in his own juices.

Some advice about when to redouble and when not:

LHO	Partner	RHO	You	♠ QJ75 ♡ 2 ◊ Q8642 ♣ 986
1♣	1♡	P	P	Redouble. Partner figures to do better in
Dbl	P	P	?	1♠ doubled or 2◊ doubled than in 1♡ doubled.

LHO	Partner	RHO	You	♠ QJ75 ♡ 2 ◊ Q8642 ♣ 986
1♠	2♡	P	P	Pass. Partner might be in worse trouble if you
Dbl	P	P	?	redoubled for rescue and he played 3♣ doubled.

Why did we pass the 2- level overcall but redouble the 1-level overcall with the same hand? One-level overcalls can be frivolous---er, we mean adventurous, but two-level overcalls show genuine SUITS and their usual six-card length means that the overcaller is more likely to be short in other suits.

The higher the level of the overcall, the poorer support you can expect for other suits, hence we recommend *against* playing SOS redoubles beyond the two-level.

Mike Lawrence offered a guideline to help decide whether to make a two-level overcall in close cases. If you intend to retreat to three of your suit after partner bids an invitational 2NT, you probably shouldn't overcall. When Mike talks, we listen, even if we sometimes disagree.

We would overcall 2♣ with ♠ A54 ♡ 3 ◊ 953 ♣ AQJ1063, 11 HCP's, but wouldn't dream of doing so with ♠ A54 ♡ Q2 ◊ Q53 ♣ AQ753, despite its 14 high-card points.

Woodrow Wilson, take your '14 points' to the peace-talk table in Versailles where they might do some good, but stay away from the bridge table.

HIGHER LEVEL REDOUBLES – BUSINESS OR SOS?

All redoubles at game level or higher are Greedy Redoubles ("I bet we can make it."). At high levels, there is seldom a safe escape hatch anyway.

West	North	East	South
4♡	P	P	Dbl
P	P	Redbl	

This redouble is *not* for rescue. South will pay a stiff price for his double when East holds something like ♠ KQ76 ♡ J ◊ A1084 ♣ AQ84.

The only potential SOS redoubles of games are of 3NT contracts and sometimes the redoubler's partner may become confused.

West	North	East	South
1♠	P	2♣	P
2NT	P	3NT	Dbl
P	P	Redbl	

This is a business redouble. South is asking for a club lead, but East may have extra values and might have been contemplating a slam try.

By contrast, these auctions require discussion even in experienced partnerships:

LHO	You	RHO	Partner
(3♣, 3◊, 3♡ or 3♠)	3NT	Dbl	Redbl

You may have nine cold tricks or have gambled under pressure of preemption. If you gambled, you may have planned to run from a double. A sensible use of this redouble is to tell you "Don't run!"

By contrast, to play this redouble as 'SOS' requires you to know where to run. Often you won't. Choice of three unbid suits? How can partner have good enough support for all three? No thanks!

West	North	East	South	
1♠	1NT*	P	3NT	*natural, unless otherwise agreed
Dbl	Redbl			

Might North have ♠ A54 ♡ A6 ◊ Q1064 ♣ AQJ4 and want South to run to his better minor? We don't think so. Not when South may have undisclosed help in spades, or a flat hand with nowhere to run. So, not that you're likely to see this auction often, North's redouble is best treated as "Don't run!"

THE LAST WORD

SOS redoubles can be very useful, but you should make them only when you are desperate, have enough length in the suits to which you ask partner to run, and are confident partner will know what you mean.

Remember, you needn't find a contract partner can make, merely a less disastrous one. But if you beef up your two-level overcalls, the opponents won't double so often and you'll require rescue less often still.

If after considering everything, you still can't tell whether a redouble is SOS or business, assume SOS. Greedy redoubles to 'gild the lily' are seldom necessary. But sometimes SOS redoubles can save you from the miry clay.

Deal # 12   Danger

You are North: ♠ 763 ♡ K82 ◊ 5 ♣ AKJ863

West	North	East	South
1♡	2♣	P	P
Dbl	P	P	Redbl
P	?		

How should you interpret South's redouble? If he couldn't stand clubs, wouldn't he have run the first time?

We don't think so. Even when playing new-suit advances as non-forcing, a sensible treatment, he needs a pretty good suit to bid 2◊ or 2♠. Neither ◊ Q10xxx nor ♠ J109xxx will hack it, but South may well have both for his redouble, which is clearly SOS here. He was hoping an opponent would bid over 2♣ to take you off the hook.

But now he's begging you to run with his SOS redouble. You might not be able to make whatever you bid, but you rate to fare much worse in 2♣ doubled. If you pass confusedly, don't be surprised to score minus 1600. Count yourself lucky to have a three-card diamond or spade suit to which to run.

Bid 2♠. You can expect to get doubled and go down---but not as much as in 2♣.

```
                         North
                         ♠ 7 6 3
                         ♡ K 8 2
                         ◊ 5
                         ♣ A K J 8 6 3
         West                              East
         ♠ A Q 2                           ♠ K 5
         ♡ A Q 10 7 6                       ♡ 5 4
         ◊ K 10 4                          ◊ A 7 6 2
         ♣ 5 2                             ♣ Q 10 9 7 4
                         South
                         ♠ J 10 9 8 4
                         ♡ J 9 3
                         ◊ Q J 9 8 3
                         ♣ void
```

At favorable vulnerability, you hold ♠ 8 ♡ KQJ107532 ◊ 4 ♣ 1043
and open 4♡. Your LHO doubles for takeout, Yes, most modern pairs use takeout doubles through 4♡ and most experts play takeout doubles through 4♠. Partner redoubles and RHO passes.

Your call? Does partner want you to run or is this a 'they made a mistake' redouble? Decide before peeking.

West
♠ Q 7 3 2
♡ 8 6 4
◊ J 8 6 3
♣ 7 5

East
♠ A K 4
♡ A
◊ Q 9 7 5
♣ K J 8 6 2

South
♠ J 10 9 6 5
♡ 9
◊ A K 10 2
♣ A Q 9

South's redouble is a business redouble. He has no reason to run for you have not been doubled for penalties. But what if your opponents use penalty doubles of 4♡ preempts? South has no reason to expect you to have any suit to which to run at this high level. That's why redoubles of opening three- and four-bids are not SOS.

South expects to supply three, more likely four winners. Had South passed, West might pass from fright, and you would score 690, with the club finesse providing an overtrick. If they let you play in 4♡ redoubled, that 690 becomes 1080.

If they run to 4♠, South will double and collect a juicy 1100 penalty.

Did you pull South's redouble, thinking it 'SOS' after RHO's sly pass? Ouch!

Now is a good time to review our *Three R's*. Then answer: how many of those five rules preclude the interpretation of South's redouble as 'SOS'? We count *five*.

Deal # 14   One After Another

Both Vul: As East, you hold ♠ void ♡ 1098742 ◊ Q109875 ♣ 6

South	West	North	East
1◊	1♠	P	P
Dbl	P	P	?

Well, that was no surprise. East should redouble to get West to pick another suit. An SOS redouble. And trust West does not pass 1♠ redoubled. The auction continues:

South	West	North	East
1◊	1♠	P	P
Dbl	P	P	Redbl
P	2♣	Dbl	?

Not a surprise either. So let's try again.

Rule: Once the SOS redoubles start, they never end.

South	West	North	East
1◊	1♠	P	P
Dbl	P	P	Redbl
P	2♣	Dbl	Redbl
P	2◊	P	P
Dbl	P	P	?

(Redbl — Not a surprise either. So let's try once more..)

Finally, a suit we can stand. By now, we are probably out of redouble cards in our bidding box. Whatever happens next is of little concern.

```
                        North
                        ♠ A K 10 7 6 4
                        ♡ J 3
                        ◊ void
                        ♣ 10 8 7 4 2
West                                          East
♠ Q J 9 8 5                                   ♠ void
♡ A                                           ♡ 10 9 8 7 4 2
◊ J 4 2             South                     ◊ Q 10 9 8 7 5
♣ A K J 9          ♠ 3 2                      ♣ 6
                   ♡ K Q 6 5
                   ◊ A K 6 3
                   ♣ Q 5 3
```

67

Deal # 15   Keep on Running

IMPs, both vul

You, North, hold ♠ 109532 ♡ J8763 ◊ 763 ♣ void

Lefty	Partner	Righty	You (North)
…	1♣	P	?

One of our favorite bridge writers once wrote that any hand with a five-card major, regardless of strength, should respond to 1♣ or 1◊.

We disagree. Want to guess partner's rebid over a 1♠ response? (a) 2♣? (b) 2◊? (c) 3♣? (d) 2NT? (e) some number of spades?

All five guesses are reasonable, but Danny forgot to include 3NT when Jim posed this as a problem. Opener might have ♠ 6 ♡ K5 ◊ A94 ♣ AKQ8743.

Wisely---or should we say, *sanely*---you pass, and the auction continues:

You hold ♠ 109532 ♡ J8763 ◊ 763 ♣ void

West	North (you)	East	South
…	…	…	1♣
P	P	Dbl	P
P	?		

Now you must run, but to which major? Did you guess hearts? Wrong! Did you guess spades? Wrong! It wouldn't help to change the ♠10 to the ♠Q, or the ♡J to the ♡K. It would still be a guess. To avoid guessing, you must redouble. A classic 'SOS' redouble!

You can't have strength when you passed 1♣. You can't have length when you didn't raise clubs or pass 1♣ doubled cheerfully. If partner runs to 1◊, you can pass, but if an opponent doubles that, you must redouble again. *Once the SOS redoubling starts, a subsequent redouble is SOS again.*

Alas, when the actual North redoubled, South mistook it for a greedy business redouble … and passed. Fortunately, no money was at stake.

As West's ♡5 opening lead hit the table, North smiled and said, "Don't make six!" He wasn't smiling when he marked -2200 on his private scoresheet for down four.

At the other table:

	♠ 109532	IMPs, both vul			
	♡ J8763	West	North	East	South
	◊ 763	…	…	…	1♣
	♣ void	P	P	Dbl	P
♠ J86	♠ AKQ4	P	Redbl	P	1◊
♡ 54	♡ KQ10	P	P	Dbl	P
◊ K8	◊ A1054	P	Redbl	P	1♡
♣ A108652	♣ J7	P	P	Dbl	P
	♠ 7	P	P		
	♡ A92				
	◊ QJ92				
	♣ KQ943				

A trump lead and good defense thereafter beat 1♡ doubled three, -800.

"Sorry," said South when his teammates came back to the table to compare scores. "I should have opened one diamond. Then they'd probably bid three notrump and make four. Lose five."

"No," said his East teammate. "We never bid anything. Plus 800. Win 16."

CHAPTER

TEN

REDOUBLES

AFTER DOUBLES

OF ARTIFICIAL

BIDS

DEAL 16

THE LAW OF HIGH LEVEL REDOUBLES

Increasingly, artificial bids have become a large component of auctions. Typically, doubles of artificial bids are lead-directing, though some conventions have been invented that treat them differently. We propose a rule to help us remember which redoubles are greedy redoubles, their natural meaning, and which have artificial meanings.

At or above the four-level, redoubles of natural bids are Greedy Redoubles and redoubles of artificial bids have artificial meanings.

Artificial four-level bids fall into two categories, bids that show some other suit or suits like transfer bids, and slam tries in an agreed suit. First let's discuss the artificial slam tries. They fall into three categories: keycard-asking auctions, splinters and cue bids, called 'control bids' by some.

KEYCARD ASKING AUCTIONS

Blackwood of some type, 4NT, is the most commonly used and abused keycard ask. However, after agreement on a particular minor suit, Roman Keycard Gerber and replies thereto have substantial merit. Other four-level suit-bids may have merit as keycard asks too.

Here's one: a 4♠ bid used to ask for keys with hearts agreed, a convention called *Kickback* for which we have Jeff Rubens to thank. This avoids a 5♠ reply to a 4NT ask when 5♡ is the limit of the deal.

If an opponent doubles a Keycard Ask, we can save steps by passing to show none or three keys, redoubling to show one or four, bidding the first step to show two without the queen of the agreed suit and the second step to show two with the queen.

For example, if a 4♣ bid that asks in diamonds is doubled, we can *pass* with no keys, redouble with one, and so forth. But note that if the asking bid is four of the trump suit itself, so that 4♣ asks in clubs, only the most foolish opponent will double, in which case this efficient system is off, and *Greedy Redoubles* apply.

He likely intends running from a redouble, so unless you hope to double a runout, you would do better to answer keys instead. You have one extra step, pass with none, bid 4♦ with one, and so forth.

Now let's consider a Roman Keycard Gerber 4♣ that asks in *diamonds*. Suppose Righty doubles partner's 4♡ reply. Now you have two extra steps: pass (instead of 4♠) to ask for the ♢Q, redouble (instead of 5♣) to ask for specific kings, 4NT or 5♢ to sign off.

REDOUBLES OF DOUBLED SPLINTERS

Splinters too fall into several categories. They can show singletons specifically, they can show voids specifically, or they can show either singletons or voids ambiguously. They can even be *displaced*. For example, in a structure Danny used several decades ago, a 4♢ response to 1♠ showed a singleton *heart*.

Many partnerships play doubles of splinters as lead directing for other suits. As previously mentioned, in a *Bridge World* article in the 1990s, Danny suggested that it ask for the highest unbid suit. Jim remembers learning this years ago as Designated Hitter, DH, double for the higher. However, if the double is not alerted, so you can assume it is calling for the lead of the short suit, a simple rule will serve you well.

Redouble to show the ace of the doubled suit. Even if, for example, a 4♢ response to 1♠ may be based on a diamond void in your system, your partner will be pleased to learn of your duplicated ♢A which may discourage him from bidding a slam.

REDOUBLES OF DOUBLED CUE BIDS ('Control Bids')

Like splinters, cue bids come in a bewildering array of sizes and shapes. Old-fashioned cue bids normally show specifically the ace of the suit unless that ace has been shown previously. The king of *partner's first suit* may be cue-bid immediately. After an ace has been cue-bid, the king of its suit then becomes cue-biddable.

Some modern 'control-bidding' styles, often referred to as Italian Cue Bids, treat aces, kings, singletons and voids as cue-biddable indiscriminately. Let's cover all styles. If a cue bid promises the ace, then a redouble shows the king. If a cue bid promises either the ace or king, then a redouble shows the other. If a cue bid may be based on shortness, then a redouble shows the ace.

REDOUBLES OF TEXAS AND SOUTH AFRICAN TRANSFERS

South African Transfers after partner opens 1NT (in some partnerships also 2NT) use a 4♣ response to show hearts and a 4♦ response to show spades. These preceded Texas Transfers, not because apartheid preceded Jim Crow, but to avoid the disasters that occurred when one partner thought 4♡ showed hearts and the other thought it showed spades.

South African was the original form of Texas, but some American expert, no doubt having been weaned on Gerber Baby Food, switched to the current form of Texas to let 4♣ be used as Gerber.

Danny was weaned on bananas, so he prefers South African, but we won't try to get you to switch. If the 2800 he scored when a redouble of 4♡ to 'retransfer' to 4♠ was passed doesn't sway you, maybe nothing will.

The first consideration when the transfer is doubled is trying to declare from the correct hand, which is often responder's. Here's a scheme that lets either partner become declarer. We'll use 1NT – pass - 4♦ - double for our example. Might you open 1NT with a diamond holding of ♦ 1073 or ♦ J102 or worse? Of course, we do so once each day and twice on Sundays.

So if responder's 4♦ transfer gets doubled, now might be a good time to let him declare four of his major. As opener, you can pass to let him bid it and do so.

But if you have the guarded ♦K or ♦AQ, you'll be happy to declare the final contract yourself, so accept the transfer.

Finally, if you have the ♦A but lack the ♦Q, your partner might have it, so in this case you should redouble to show the ♦A and let responder declare, putting the doubler on lead.

In sum, after a Texas or South African Transfer (for example, 4◊) is doubled:

(a) Opener passes to deny having the ◊AQ or ◊Kx. Responder can bid his major himself, perhaps he has the ◊K.

    ** Redouble by responder is a retransfer.

(b) Opener accepts the transfer with a tenace, ◊Kx or ◊AQx.

(c) Opener redoubles to show the ◊A without the ◊Q; perhaps responder has the ◊Q and will benefit from a diamond lead as declarer.

WHERE AND WHEREFOR ART THOU, OSWALD?

The merits of both Texas and South African Transfers are overblown, but the merits of Jacoby Transfers are underblown.

After a 4♡ Texas Transfer, and opener's mandatory 4♠ acceptance, responder can invoke Roman Keycard Blackwood by rebidding 4NT, but that's about all that Texas adds to Jacoby Transfers. Occasionally, there is some preemptive value in jumping immediately.

But after a Jacoby Transfer, 1NT-2♡; 2♠, responder has oodles of bidding space in which to anchor spades as trump and move towards slam.

Unlike a 4◊ or 4♡ transfer, a doubled 2◊ or 2♡ transfer bid can sometimes be redoubled by opener to suggest playing there. Without this prospect, an enterprising opponent can double a Jacoby Transfer for the lead at the drop of a hat.

Just as after a double of a 4◊ transfer, opener may rather be dummy than declarer, especially with holdings like ◊ 976 or ◊ A53.

Here are two ways to play the redouble after a Jacoby transfer is doubled. Jim likes one, Danny likes the other. Or you may have your own. But this is an area fraught with danger. Don't be surprised to see -1600 or -2800 at times.

Danny's Method:

There are *natural* meanings of opener's calls after 1NT-pass-2◊-double:

(a) Redouble suggests playing there ("Perhaps they made a mistake!"),

(b) Pass says, "I'd rather be dummy to perhaps protect responder's guarded king of diamonds, or doubleton queen opposite opener's ace-third against a lead through you."

(c) 2♡ simply accepts the transfer and lets the auction proceed normally,

(d) 3♡ super-accepts the transfer. Five-card heart support, or four-card heart support with a ruffing value, can turn what was originally a 17 *high-card-point* hand into a 19 *support-point* hand.

If opener passes the double of 2◊, or redoubles, responder will often have a garden variety weak hand, in which case he can bid 2♡, normally ending the auction. With enough to bid or invite a game, responder can make the rebid he intended to make over an accepted transfer, or pass opener's redouble.

Sometimes, however, responder will have a pretty good hand with diamonds as well as hearts. Then he will do well to redouble *to suggest playing there*, the natural meaning of this redouble. Natural is a good default when you have no partnership agreement to the contrary.

Natural isn't always best, however. It is merely what applies in the absence of partnership agreements to play conventions. Might there be something better? Jim thinks so after a double of a Jacoby Transfer.

Jim's Method:

Take advantage of the extra bidding space to show degree of support for responder's major. Thus, after a double of a Jacoby Transfer:

(a) Opener accepts the transfer with normal three-card support or better.

(b) Opener redoubles to suggest playing there ("they made a mistake!").

(c) Opener passes with poor support, such as a doubleton or weak tripleton.

Then responder has these options:

   (c1) He can redouble to re-transfer and continue the auction normally.

   (c2) He can bid a new suit to suggest playing there. For example, with ♠ Q8643 ♡ 84 ◊ 8 ♣ KJ532 or ♠ Q8643 ♡ 84 ◊ KJ532 ♣ 8 he can infer poor spade support from opener's pass of his Jacoby Transfer, and bid a nonforcing 3♣ or 3◊ to propose playing there.

Danny applauds this feature of Jim's Method.

   (c3) He can bid 2NT or 3NT directly, without re-transferring, to deny a stopper in the doubled suit.

   (c4) He can redouble to re-transfer. If he bids after opener accepts the re-transfer, new suits are forcing and notrump bids show a stopper.

REDOUBLE WHEN STAYMAN IS DOUBLED

When you open 1NT and partner invokes Stayman, it's not unusual for your RHO to double for a club lead. You'll do well to have firm partnership agreements.

After 1NT – P – 2♣ - Dbl

Just as over a Jacoby Transfer, opener should be able to make a natural "Let's play here!" redouble. What does responder need to sit for this 'business' redouble?

That depends on both his hand strength and his club length.

With game values, he can pass 2♣ redoubled even with a singleton club.

With invitational values, he needs at least a doubleton.

And with a weak hand, perhaps with five spades and four hearts planning to rebid 2♠ over opener's 2♦ but pass a major suit reply, he needs at least three clubs.

But opener will seldom want to make a business redouble. What then? Again, there are various methods and Jim and Danny each have their favorites.

Danny says "If an opponent wants clubs to be led against our major-suit contract, make him lead them himself!" Danny favors a convention he calls *Jujitsu*, based on the theory that it is usually best for responder to be declarer. Even when opener has a club stopper or two.

Should ♣K3 make opener want to declare? No, as responder may have ♣Q107. Should ♣A64 or ♣AJ4 make opener want to declare? No, as responder may have ♣Q3. Should ♣AQ4 make opener want to declare? No, as responder may have ♣J5.

Therefore opener should *transfer* to his lowest-ranking four-card major. With no major, opener passes. When he does, this gives responder a chance to make a business redouble of 2♣.

With hearts or both majors, opener bids 2◊. With spades but not hearts, opener bids 2♡. Responder learns of opener's suits first and can bid 3♣ next if he wants to ask about opener's club stoppers.

Smolen, a convention we love, does *not* apply, but *Reverse Smolen* does. Over opener's pass, no four-card major, responder bids three of his *five-card* major with a game-going 5-4 or 4-5 in the majors.

If responder cares to ask for a club stopper with 3♣, opener bids 3◊ to deny a club stopper, but with a club stopper he bids 3♡ (three *spades*), 3♠ (three *hearts*), or 3NT (3-3 in the majors).

Jim likes Danny's method but prefers a different method for casual partnerships.

1)With a club stopper, opener is happy to declare and makes his normal reply to Stayman. Of course, opener may make a business redouble.

2)Without a club stopper, opener *passes*. Then responder redoubles as *Reverse Stayman* in an attempt to make himself declarer, putting the doubler on opening lead, as responder may have a club stopper.

In reply to Reverse Stayman, opener bids 2◊ with no four-card major, 2♥ with four SPADES, 2♠ with four HEARTS, and 2NT with two four-card majors. And of course, Smolen does *not* apply.

Frivolous doubles of Stayman can sometimes backfire. For an example of what can happen, even to the best players, see Deal # 15 at the end of this chapter.

DOUBLES AND REDOUBLES OF COMPLETELY ARTIFICIAL BIDS.

What about doubling other artificial bids, such as opener's 2◊ reply to Stayman or a neutral 2◊ response to a strong artificial 2♣ opening? Let's see what can happen. Take a look at the two deals on the following pages.

THE MAMMOTH AND THE WHALE

Homo sapiens isn't the only mammal on the planet. A zoologist who refuses to be identified further recognizes two other species, the Mammoth and the Whale.

The Mammoth is a very strong balanced hand, shown in modern bidding methods by an artificial 2♣ opening. The usual neutral response is 2◊ followed by a 2NT rebid, which may be passed only when responder is virtually broke.

The Whale is a still stronger balanced hand, shown similarly except that opener insists on reaching game or slam by jumping to 3NT over the usual 2◊ response. However, by now, most experts have adopted *Kokish*, the brainchild of Eric Kokish, an expert with an encyclopedic knowledge of bidding.

Instead of jumping to 3NT, consuming a full level of precious bidding space, opener bids a Kokish (or as Eric modestly calls it, *Birthright*) 2♡, which shows either a Whale or a monster heart hand. Then responder normally bids 2♠, so that opener can clarify by bidding 2NT, game forcing, a Whale, or anything else implying hearts.

Danny's variation ('Kleinish') lets responder bid 2NT over 2♡ with long spades (letting the Whale bid 3♠ to become declarer) or three of any lower suit with a "natural positive" in that suit, as the declarership has already been determined.

We advise strongly against standing in front of the headlights of either huge beast.

In a National Knockout Teams championship (November 2022) two brave primates ventured into the stomping grounds of the Mammoth and the deep waters of the Whale with lead directing doubles.

Let's see how a Mammoth defended his neck of the forest when a primate invaded.

After two passes, the Mammoth (North, his usual habitat) opened 2♣ on favorable vulnerability and received the usual neutral 2◊ response. Put yourself in the Striped-Tail Ape's place holding ♠ 103 ♡ QJ32 ◊ KJ964 ♣ Q2.

He doubled. The Mammoth was just a baby Mammoth, but he knew enough to redouble with ♠ AK975 ♡ AK ◊ AQ108 ♣ J10. Responder had values enough to sit for it, ♠ Q654 ♡ 1098 ◊ 52 ♣ A975. With finesses working and suits splitting, he scored all of dummy's trumps and five top tricks in the other suits, +760.

The Ape might have won 5 IMPs had his teammates bid the 6♠ they made on the actual favorable layout, but without a double of 2◊ to guide them, they got lost in the forest and stopped in 4♠ for a 7-IMP loss.

We wonder: From where did the Ape expect to get the six tricks needed to beat 2◊? Why was he eager to get a diamond lead when he had honors in two other suits? And to where did he think he could run from a redouble?

In another match at the same event, an Ape tried to swim in a Whale's deep Arctic waters. The Whale (North) opened 2♣ in third seat on favorable vulnerability and rebid a Kokish 2♡ over the Dolphin's (South's) neutral 2◊ response. The Dolfin bid 2♠ as requested.

The Ape had ♠ AJ874 ♡ 103 ◊ 974 ♣ J74 and mumbled something in Australopithecanese that Danny eventually translated as "They're playing my song." Then the Ape placed the double card he had been grasping in his tail upon an ice floe directly in front of the Whale.

The Whale's pass suggested that he had---well, a Whale. The Dolphin flipped his redouble card in the air, and 2♠ redoubled became the final contract.

The Monkey (East) waited patiently, then blurted out "Abba dabba dabba," which in monkey-talk means "It's your lead, partner."

Heeding his own lead-directing double, the Ape led the ♠A and saw:

```
                    ♠ K 10
                    ♡ A 8
                    ◊ A K Q 10
                    ♣ A K Q 9 3
  ♠ A J 8 7 4
  ♡ 10 3
  ◊ 9 7 4
  ♣ J 7 4
                    ♠ Q 9 6 3
                    ♡ Q 9 7 2
                    ◊ 6
                    ♣ 10 6 5 2
```

Yes, he had brought his periscope with him, but it didn't help. He shifted to the ♡10, ducked to the Monkey's ♡K. After winning the heart continuation in dummy, the Dolphin cashed dummy's ♠K and six top tricks in the minors to reach a three-card ending. The Ape was forced to ruff the next trick, the third for the defense, but then had to lead from his remaining ♠J8 up to the Dolphin's ♠Q9.

Two spades redoubled with two overtricks cost the Ape 1040 points. an 11-IMP loss for his team, as his teammates stopped in game. Danny translated the last words the Ape mumbled in Australopithecanese as "I thought I had until April fifteenth to file my tax return."

> "Orangutans are skeptical of changes in their cages."
> ---Paul Simon, *At the Zoo*

Some lessons from the Zookeeper:

(1) Don't step in front of a Mammoth or swim in front of a Whale.

(2) Don't make low-level lead-directing doubles against *unlimited* opponents.

(3) Avoid low-level lead-directing doubles without a *third honor* in the suit.

(4) Don't make lead-directing doubles if you'd be happy with partner's leads in the other suits.

(5) Don't make low-level lead-directing doubles when you have no idea what the final contract will be nor who will declare it.

(6) The lower the bid, the better suit you need for a lead-directing double.

(7) Never double a bid for the lead if you know you can't beat it.

Deal # 16   Turning the Cube

In backgammon, the doubling cube may be turned indefinitely to increase the stakes, and its six sides are numbered 2, 4, 8, 16, 32 and 64 accordingly. Jim once played in a money "bridge" game altered to permit unlimited redoubles similarly.

While the highest of "high-rollers" was in the washroom, the others rigged a deal to give him ♠ AQJ1098765432 ♡ K ◊ void ♣ void. After a series of re-redoubles that drove the cube to 64 in 6♠, Mr. Highroller smiled at his LHO and said, "It's your lead, but I think I can claim."

"Let's just play it out," said Lefty, sliding the ♡2 onto the table. You know the rest.

Danny refuses to let Jim name the old friend of his who sat West on this deal from a recent National Team Championship:

```
        ♠ 9 5 3              IMPs, none vul
        ♡ A K 3
        ◊ K 7 2              West  North  East   South
        ♣ K J 10 7                 1NT*   P      2♣^    *14-16 HCP
♠ 10 8            ♠ Q J 7 4  Dbl   Redbl  All    Pass   ^ Stayman
♡ Q 2            ♡ J 8 6 5 4
◊ A 10 8 6       ◊ Q J 9 3   East could have lived with 2♣ doubled,
♣ A 8 6 5 4      ♣ void      but redouble? He probably wanted to pull
        ♠ A K 6 2            a re-redouble card to get East to bid, but
        ♡ 10 9 7             couldn't find one so he passed. South
        ◊ 5 4                also wanted to 'turn the cube' but he
        ♣ Q 9 3 2            passed, licking his lips.
```

East led the ♣A and another club. South overtook dummy's ♣10 with the ♣Q and led the ◊4. East ducked, dummy's ◊K won, and a second diamond let West win the ◊10 and lead a third club. Declarer finished with one diamond, three clubs, one diamond ruff, and four top tricks in the majors to make an overtrick. + 760.

At the other table, North-South overbid to 3NT and went down. Note the importance of having business redoubles on opener's palette to punish "How dare you bid my five-card suit!" doubles like this one.

Oh, the doubler of 6♠ on Jim's 64-cube deal had two singletons: the ♡2 and ♠K. His partner won the ♡A and led another heart for the doubler to overruff declarer.

CHAPTER

ELEVEN

THE BIG SWING

Remember when you were a kid sitting on a swing yelling "higher, higher?" Well, here is a big swing in bridge. How does going from plus 1000 to minus 840 sound? And at the one or two level to boot! Think it can't happen? Watch and tell us what you would do.

Hand # 1: You have your usual ♠ 9643 ♡ 874 ◊ 875 ♣ 1064

Righty	You	Lefty	Partner
1♠	P	2♠	Dbl
Redbl	?		

What's the problem? Why not pass and let partner pick a suit? Take a look at Hand # 2 and you'll see.

Hand # 2: This time you have ♠ AQ1097 ♡ 106 ◊ Q54 ♣ 753

The same auction but now you pass and want partner to pass also. Hmmm. With Hand #1, you wanted partner to rescue himself. With Hand #2 you hoped he'd pass.

Are you playing with a mind reader? In these situations, if you get it right, plus 600 or 1000. If you're wrong, probably minus 640 or 840. What's it going to be?

Here is a simple agreement that we think will help. If the bidding is at the 2-level, passing says you want to defend. What about the 1-level?

The meaning of your pass depends on your position. If you're behind the opponent who showed a five-card suit, your pass over his redouble is a penalty pass. But if you're in front of him, your pass over his redouble asks partner to pull to the suit of his choice.

With Hand #1 you needed to bid. As your only four-bagger was the opponent's suit, you should bid 2NT. Unless you're playing with a pinochle deck, there's no chance you're bidding it to make. Instead, you're begging partner to rescue himself. Here is a different example.

Righty	You	Lefty	Partner
1♠	Dbl	Redbl	P

Partner is in front of the spade bidder, so his pass asks you to rescue yourself. But look at the difference here:

Righty	You	Lefty	Partner
1♠	P	P	Dbl
Redbl	?	You are behind the spade bidder. If you pass, it's for penalty.	

Try this quiz. What is the last pass in each auction? Answers on the next page.

(1)
Righty	You	Lefty	Partner
1♣	P	2♣	Dbl
Redbl	P		

(2)
You	Lefty	Partner	Righty	
1♣	1♠	Dbl*	Redbl	* Negative Dbl (♡)
P				

(3)
Righty	You	Lefty	Partner
1♣	Dbl	Redbl	P

(4)
Lefty	Partner	Righty	You
1♡	P	P	Dbl
Redbl	P		

(5)
Partner	Righty	You	Lefty
1◊	2♣	P	P
Dbl	Redbl	P	

(6)
Righty	You	Lefty	Partner
1◊	P	1♡	Dbl
Redbl	P		

(7)
You	Lefty	Partner	Righty	
1♣	1♡	Dbl*	Redbl	* Negative Dbl (four ♠)
P				

(8)
Righty	You	Lefty	Partner
1◊	P	P	Dbl
Redbl	P		

(1)	Righty	You	Lefty	Partner	
	1♠	P	2♠	Dbl	
	Redbl	P			Penalty (behind ♠ bidder)
(2)	You	Lefty	Partner	Righty	
	1♣	1♠	Dbl*	Redbl	* Negative Dbl (♡)
	P				Takeout, denying hearts
					In front of ♠ bidder
(3)	Righty	You	Lefty	Partner	
	1♠	Dbl	Redbl	P	Rescue yourself
					In front of ♠ bidder
(4)	Lefty	Partner	Righty	You	
	1♡	P	P	Dbl	Penalty
	Redbl	P			Behind ♡ bidder
(5)	Partner	Righty	You	Lefty	
	1◊	2♣	P	P	Penalty
	Dbl	Redbl	P		Behind ♣ bidder
(6)	Righty	You	Lefty	Partner	
	1◊	P	1♡	Dbl	Rescue yourself
	Redbl	P			In front of ♡ bidder
(7)	You	Lefty	Partner	Righty	
	1♣	1♡	Dbl*	Redbl	* Negative Dbl (four ♠)
	P				Takeout, denying four ♠
					In front of ♡ bidder
(8)	Righty	You	Lefty	Partner	
	1◊	P	P	Dbl	Penalty
	Redbl	P			Behind ◊ bidder

CHAPTER TWELVE

REDOUBLES AFTER THE OPPONENTS OPEN

DEAL 17

When the opponents open, they have started exchanging information before you have. As your redouble gives the opponents extra room to exchange more information, you should redouble only with strong defense, and simply raise partner with a fit.

Let's look at some examples:

RHO	You	LHO	Partner	
1♣	P	1♡	1♠	
Dbl*	Redbl			*Support Double (three hearts)

Your redouble is an *anchor* redouble showing a good hand, just as it would if partner had opened 1♠. You might have ♠ 54 ♡ AJ95 ◊ Q86 ♣ KQ42, a good hand without appropriate shape to have entered over 1♣. As partner has shown values by entering between two bidders, this is a 'buy it or belt it' auction.

RHO	You	LHO	Partner
1◊	Dbl	P	1♡
Dbl	Redbl		

Your redouble is an 'oomph' redouble showing a strong hand with only three hearts. With a fourth heart you would have raised or jump-raised hearts.
Had opener passed, you probably would have cue-bid 2◊.

RHO	You	LHO	Partner
1♡	2◊	P	P
Dbl	Redbl		

Another 'oomph' redouble, but possibly a risky one, as your LHO may have passed initially with a diamond stack. So, you need both a very good suit *and* extra values. If you'd been playing Strong Single-Jump Overcalls, you might have jumped to 3◊ at your first turn. You show defense and will be happy if partner can double the runout. You might hold ♠ AQ ♡ 54 ◊ AKJ1087 ♣ K107.

In the last two auctions, you have shown a strong hand, but the deal does not necessarily belong to your side, as partner has not shown any signs of life. You might have even more than we've suggested, but unless partner springs to life, you may be through.

As East you hold ♠ A9752 ♡ KQJ94 ◊ 93 ♣ 3. The auction begins:

North	East	South	West
1♣	2♣*	Dbl	P	*majors
P	?		

What are you going to do? What does partner's pass mean? If West had a preference for one of the majors he most likely would have bid some number of hearts or spades. Does he want you to choose a major or pass?

Can you feel some tension at the table?
It's important to have an agreement. How should *pass* differ from *redouble*? We both have strong feelings about this---in opposite directions.

Jim wants a pass to say, "Let's play in 2♣ doubled!" and a redouble to be SOS asking partner to pick the major. This follows the principle that we never want to play in low level redoubled contracts

The opposite agreement is possible: *business* redoubles with a *pass* asking the Michaels Cue-Bidder to bid his better major.

West may have ♠ 8 ♡ 7 ◊ K854 ♣ KJ108642

2♣ doubled may not be a great success but rates to be better than 2♡ or 2♠ doubled on a 5-1 fit. 2♣ doubled will likely be down one or two but with careless defense, who knows how cheaply partner will get off?

Jim shows a layout with North having ♣ Axx and South having ♣ Qx, His method works out well. Danny thinks it more likely that South has a low singleton and North has ♣ AQxx. Or maybe ♣ AQ9x?

Danny suggests the opposite agreement. "Let's play here!" he prefers as the natural meaning of redouble and by passing the double, West tells East "Rescue yourself!"

But it doesn't matter what you play. Any agreement is better than no agreement. That's the stuff of which huge minuses are made. Accidents *will* happen.

CHAPTER

THIRTEEN

REDOUBLES

AFTER THEIR

NOTRUMPS

AND OURS

At last count, there were 1,594,323 different Notrump Defenses. We can't cover nearly all here. Two of the most popular are *Hamilton* and DON'T. Each features a 2♣ overcall that promises one of three or four different hand types. Under the usual pressure from partner to "Do what everybody else does!" you probably play one of those two.

LHO	Partner	RHO	You	*Penalty (how dare they try to nail us,
1NT	2♣	Dbl*	?	most opponents play it as 'Stayman'!)

For DONTers: 2♣ shows clubs and another suit. So:

Pass: "There's at least one other suit I dislike more than clubs, so you'd better not run lest you hit it. Let's play here."

Any new suit: "I don't care what your suits are, let's play in mine."

Redouble: "I hate clubs. Run to your other suit. I know you have one."

For Hamiltonians: 2♣ shows an unspecified one-suiter. The natural interpretation of your call here is:

Pass: "Let's play in your suit. Pass if it's clubs, else bid it."
Any new suit: "I don't care what your suit is, let's play in mine."
Redouble (rare): "I love clubs, please don't run."

One of Danny's hobbies over the years was devising modifications of *Hamilton.* Here's for anyone who plays *Minor-Suit Hamilton*, in which double shows clubs and 2♣ shows diamonds, each perhaps with a higher suit that intervenor plans to bid next:

First thank your RHO for doubling! Then:

Pass: "I know you don't have clubs, but let's play here anyway. I have more clubs than you have in your golf bag."
2◊:   "Let's play here. If you have a major, I don't want to hear about it."
2♡ or 2♠: "I don't care about your suits, let's play in mine."
Redouble: "Bid your major if you have one, else bid two diamonds."

WHEN THEY DOUBLE OUR NOTRUMP

Whether our opponents play old-fashioned penalty doubles, or modern artificial doubles of our 1NT openings as we recommend, we may face danger. Even artificial doubles of 1NT can be passed for penalties.

You may have noticed that if we play Minor-Suit Hamilton, we thanked the opponent who doubled our 2♣ overcall for doubling. Why? Because he gave our partner an additional option, the *redouble.* Doubles of our notrump openings give us *two* additional options.

Let us explain. Did you ever notice that the official ACBL convention cards are *biased*? By listing various conventions and for us simply to check or not, they nudge us towards adopting those conventions.

For example, in the section for notrump bidding, the ACBL lists *Lebensohl*. Consequently. some pairs who might otherwise adopt a superior alternative use *Lebensohl* instead. The relevant nudge in this case is the line marked 'System on over ___.' Many pairs 'double' some also '2♣' on that line. Here's what's wrong with that.

Stayman is a fine and dandy convention. Just try playing without it! Danny may be the last bridge player alive ever to have done so, and wouldn't want to do so again. But like any other convention, it should not be played without a full understanding of why.

On many deals, a four-four fit in a major suit plays better than notrumps, and Stayman lets us probe for such a fit while trying for a notrump game or slam. Yes, there are other uses for Stayman to get out in a major with weak hands, but they comprise a small minority of Stayman auctions.

An opposing double reduces the frequency of hands for Stayman dramatically. If the double shows high cards, responder won't be looking for game in a 4-4 fit in a major. If the double is artificial, based on suits and shape, 4-4 fits will usually play worse than notrumps, as suits figure to split badly.

So after our 1NT is doubled, we have little use for Stayman. Nor have we much need for a Greedy Redouble. A Greedy Redouble not only lets the doubler run if he doubled with a long suit, but warns the doubler's partner to run when he's in doubt. Given the wide range of penalty doubles of 1NT, the doubler's partner often runs when unbeknownst to him, the doubler has 1NT beaten in his own hand, or passes when 1NT makes.

This suggests a simple set of responses after 1NT-double. Everything is a transfer. It's especially important to have the opening lead come from the opponent with the strong hand up to opener, instead of through opener's strength up to the doubler's.

Redouble shows clubs, 2♣ shows diamonds, 2◊ shows hearts, 2♡ shows spades.

You hold ♠ KJ5 ♡ 2 ◊ 9864 ♣ J8652. Partner deals and opens 1NT.

(a) What should you do if your right-hand opponent passes?
(b) What should you do if he doubles?

(a) Pass. Even if you have a way to transfer to 3♣. To transfer to a minor, you need either a sixth card, or slam-try values with only five.
(b) Redouble -clubs. Thank you for letting us escape cheaply!

You can add to this simple structure. but you need extra shape to do so, as you'll land at the three-level. Here is *Kobe*, which applies transfers to two-suiters.

With spades and a minor, bid 2♡ to transfer to 2♠, then continue with 2NT to show clubs or 3♣ to show diamonds. Opener may accept the transfer to the minor or correct to spades, perhaps even to 4♠. Bidding *game* after Lefty has doubled 1NT?
Yes, as many modern Notrump Defenses do not include *penalty* doubles but use doubles to show other things. You can show other two-suiters in a logical order (cheaper bids show lower suits): 2♠ shows both minors, 2NT shows clubs and hearts, 3♣ shows diamonds and hearts, 3◊ shows both majors.

But *Kobe* has other applications. You can use it as your own *Notrump Defense*: 1NT- double now shows clubs. You can use it as a defense against a *Big Club*: a 1NT overcall now shows clubs. And you can add *Shaq*: a double of 1♣ remains a takeout double showing the other three suits, while 1◊, 1♡ and 1♠ overcalls also show the *other three suits*.

CHAPTER FOURTEEN

VARIOUS OTHER TYPES OF REDOUBLES

DEALS 18 – 19

ROSENKRANZ REDOUBLES

To distinguish weak support from strong, a raise with a high honor when partner overcalls and your RHO makes a Negative Double, the late George Rosenkranz of Mexico City invented the redouble that bears his name.

To show a high honor (ace, king or queen) in partner's suit, you redouble. Any other call, even a jump raise, shows at best jack-high support. Like many other conventions, Rosenkranz Redoubles sprout variations. Some exclude the queen. Others require three-card or longer support.

We advise against adopting Rosenkranz Redoubles. Not only do they carry the usual risk of crossed wires when you are playing one version and partner is playing another, but they are *anti-preemptive.*

LHO	Partner	RHO	You	
1♣	1♡	Dbl*	Redbl**	*Negative **Rosenkranz

A typical hand would be ♠ 975 ♡ K73 ◊ A8642 ♣ 87

Do you see why we dislike this convention? The auction may continue:

LHO	Partner	RHO	You	
1♣	1♡	Dbl*	Redbl**	*Negative **Rosenkranz
2♣	2♡	3♣	All pass	

… when without *Rosenkranz* your simple 2♡ raise might end the auction.

Guildenstern's Law: "No convention that replaces a simple raise is worth playing."

We prefer to redouble just as we redouble after a takeout double of our partner's opening bids; *anchor redoubles* to show strong hands with good defense, or if followed by support, game-invitational or better three-card raises.

SUPPORT REDOUBLES

Many pairs play *Support Doubles*. After you make a 1♡ or 1♠ response and the next player bids, opener's raise of your major promises four-card support while his double shows three-card support.

Most users of Support Doubles treat opener's doubles differently when the response to 1♣ is 1♢ and the next player bids 1♠; they double to show *four hearts*.

Support Redoubles are similar when opener's RHO doubles, and most devotees of Support Doubles play them also. After a takeout double of a 1-level response, opener's raise to two promises four cards while his redouble shows three-card support.

Though Eric Rodwell invented the convention, it was Danny who wrote *Twenty Questions about Support Doubles* in the June 2000 *Bridge World*. If there are only two answers to each question, there are approximately 1,048,576 versions. In a recent attempt to form a partnership with another expert, Danny spent hours on the phone discussing in just what auctions they would use Support Doubles.

If there are any better bridge players than Eric Rodwell (there may be none), they might be Zia Mahmoud and Michael Rosenberg, who had a fine partnership a few decades ago. Once Danny had the pleasure of watching them in a national championship match. Zia was playing one version, Michael another. They messed up royally. As Mr. Micawber said, "Result: misery."

If that doesn't dissuade you from playing Support Doubles and Redoubles, reread Guildenstern's Law. However, just in case you're a Dedicated Follower of Fashion:

You	Lefty	Partner	RHO
1♣	P	1♥	Dbl
	or		
1♣	1♡	1♠	Dbl (any meaning)

If you play Support Redoubles, any raise of partner's major promises four cards and a redouble shows three-card support, regardless of strength or shape. Some addicts say that a pass or any other bid denies as many as three cards in responder's suit, but that's one of the 20 questions to be discussed.

Much as we like good trump spot cards, 98.6 is merely normal body temperature, not normal *support*. So with three *weak* cards, opener needn't use the convention; he may still pass or bid.

Deal # 18   Another Type of Redouble

	North	East	South	West
♠ K J 4	1◇	P	1♠	Dbl
♡ A Q 6 5	Redbl*	1NT	2◇	3♣
◇ Q 10 5 2	All	Pass		
♣ 6 3				

♠ 10 7	♠ A Q 8 6
♡ K J 3 2	♡ 10 9
◇ 6 4	◇ K 8 3
♣ A K 10 9 8	♣ J 7 5 2.

*Support Redouble

```
          ♠ 9 5 3 2
          ♡ 8 7 4
          ◇ A J 9 7
          ♣ Q 4
```

(1) What kind of hand would you think opener had if he passed West's double?
(2) What kind of hand would you think opener had if he rebid 1NT?

To both we answer, a balanced minimum. So why two calls for one hand?

Instead, pass with a balanced minimum and poor support. Raise with high-honor third and a ruffing value. Bid a "Support 1NT" with high-honor third and extras. That leaves opener's redouble as an *anchor* redouble.

A sensible South would raise 1◇ to 2◇, shutting out a 2♣ overcall and *buying the contract.* West would pass, fearing that a double would fetch 2♠ from East.

Danny plays neither Support Doubles nor Support Redoubles. He plays Support Raises and says, "Never bid a four-card major if you will cringe in terror when partner raises on high-honor-third with a ruffing value."

Kleinman's Law (with a nod to Bob Hamman): "If a simple raise is one of your options, make one!"

From the website of one of bridge's most well-known writers: "In all my years of teaching … I've never seen a convention that causes more brain freeze and confusion than Support Doubles. Players constantly forget to use them, … forget to realize partner has used them and forget the negative inferences. I recommend this convention only for players with strong concentration abilities…."

'BOP' DOUBLES

Well-known bridge teacher and writer Mel Colchamiro wrote an excellent article in the ACBL Bulletin, February, 2010. He wrote that "Please Don't Let Me Be Misunderstood," a rock song by the Animals from 1965, could be the cry of the misunderstood redouble.

Who put the BOP in the "Bop-chu-wop-chu-wop"? We suspect it was Mel, who uses it to mean *balance of power*. A redouble of an opposing takeout double says we have it. It suggests defending with the added inference that the redoubler has at best secondary support for his partner's suit. Three-card support for partner's major or four-card support for his partner's minor is always a possibility.

Long-time ACBL Bulletin columnist Jerry Helms also uses the phrase 'balance of power' in his excellent review of redoubles in the January 2014 issue. All subsequent doubles by either partner are penalty.

With game-invitational one-suiters, we like invitational jumps over intervening doubles, e.g. 1♡ - double - 3♣ with ♠ 42 ♡ K6 ◊ 852 ♣ AKJ972 and 1♡ - double - 2♣, non-forcing, with weaker hands like such as ♠ 42 ♡ 63 ◊ 852 ♣ AQJ972. The auction won't always go tamely if to show a good hand with clubs you must bid:

Partner	RHO	You	LHO
1♡	Dbl	Redbl	P
P	1♠	2♣	

Sometimes an opponent will bid 3♠. Then what?

With ♠ 42 ♡ 63 ◊ 852 ♣ AQJ972, we'd bid 2♣ over the double non-forcing

There are also BOP doubles that act like redoubles.

99

Consider these auctions:

Partner	RHO	You	
1♠	2NT*	?	*"unusual" for the two lowest unbid suits

You might hold ♠ 65 ♡ K985 ◇ Q75 ♣ AJ98. Double to show the BOP and hope of doubling the runout for penalties.

Partner	RHO	You	
1♡	2♥*	?	*spades and an unspecified minor

You might hold ♠ KJ75 ♡ 85 ◇ AQ852 ♣ 103. Double to show the BOP and hope of doubling the runout for penalties.

In each case, your double shows at least 10+ HCP, no fit for opener's suit and a desire to penalize. These are normal minimums.

What does your double sound like?

"Bop-chu-wop-chu-wop!" Yes, exactly like a redouble. BOP!

LHO	Partner	RHO	You	
1♣	1♠	Dbl*	Redbl	*Negative Double

"Dit-di-dit-di-dit"---ditto! Just like …

LHO	Partner	RHO	You
P	1♠	Dbl	Redbl

So, what's the difference between *anchor* and 'BOP? Well, Mel, we don't need to tell *you*. It's like the difference between Katie Couric and Catherine Zeta-Jones. Isn't the song "Here he comes, he's Cathy's clown!" about you?

Experienced partnerships have added a few extra gadgets that despite their complexity can be a useful addition to your partnership agreements.

One is a *worry* redouble.

1♣	P	1♠	P
1NT	P	3NT	Dbl

This double is a lead-directing double that begs for a lead in dummy's first suit, here spades. A redouble by opener shows a low doubleton and begs responder to run if he too is worried about spades.

Some play that a redouble by responder shows worry about spades and asks opener to run unless he has an honor, even a low honor, to help stop the suit.

Run? Run where? Sing along with the Beatles as they describe the *Nowhere Man*: "Knows not where he's going to."

But we do know that a Greedy Redouble can be profitable. If responder has ♠ 109xxx and substantial extras, the doubler will be sorry---especially if he doubled on ♠ AKQJxx and his partner has no spade to lead.

Here's a much better use for a *worry redouble*:

1♠	3♠	P	3NT
Dbl	Redbl		

As played by most experts, a jump cue-bid overcall in a minor is natural, showing a long running suit. But a jump cue-bid overcall in a major shows a running suit and begs partner to convert to 3NT with a stopper in opener's suit. Advancer can make a worry redouble to say that he's broke except in opener's major. The jump cue-bidder *will* know where to run to---if necessary.

The default for redoubles of 3NT, however, is *greed*.

1◇	2♣	2NT	P
3NT	P	P	Dbl

Presumably the opening leader doubled to remind himself to lead clubs. But opener knows that responder has clubs stopped and has enough strength outside to expect an overtrick or two.

In the following auction, opener would normally bid 3NT with a spade stopper, something else without one. Overcaller's double gives opener other options, including a *partial-stopper redouble*.

1♦	P	1♡	2♠
P	P	3♠	Dbl

Opener can still bid 3NT if he has a spade stopper, but now he can pass without one. A sensible partnership agreement lets him redouble to show a partial spade stopper, ♠ K, ♠ Qx, ♠ Jxx, or ♠ 10xxx.

Do you and your partner have any agreement about 'blind' doubles of 3NT? Some pairs do and must alert those doubles when they make them. For example, suppose a pair plays this double as demanding a club lead:

1NT	P	3NT	Dbl
?			

If you play *partial-stopper redoubles,* that's what opener's redouble shows here. Responder will know whether to run. Opener's pass shows either a full stopper or none, and compels responder to make a worry redouble without a full stopper. Then opener will know whether to pass or scramble.

But without an agreement to play *partial-stopper redoubles*, Greedy Redoubles apply. Yes, opener can have a fine maximum, and responder can have substantial extra values.

For an excellent in-depth discussion of this topic, read Karen Walker's discussion in the ACBL *Bulletin* November and December, 2004. You can find it in the *Bulletin* archives at www.acbl.org.

Note: These are the redoubles of which thousand-point disasters are made. Don't try them with anyone except a world-class partner with whom you've played for at least a decade. Danny plans to try them after he ends his other careers as bull-fighter, rock-climber, and sky-diver.

THE SCRAMBLING REDOUBLE

Most of us are all familiar with scrambling 2NT as two places to play, often used in balancing situations.

Well, not all of us are familiar with it. Danny isn't. In which century did he say he was born---the sixteenth or the seventeenth?

Sometimes 1NT can be a scramble if you like.

For example, here's an expert trick when you can't have enough high card points for a natural 1NT. Your hand is:

♠ 7532 ♡ 8 ♢ 10874 ♣ J953

LHO	Partner	RHO	You
1♠	Dbl	Redbl	?

You don't want to pass and have partner run to 2♡, but which minor should you choose? You can't have enough points for a true 1NT, a constructive bid. There were still only 40 HCP in the deck the last time we checked.

So bid 1NT, knowing you will be doubled. Then you can redouble to 'scramble.' With ♠ KQ ♡ Q975 ♢ A65 ♣ KQ86, partner will bid 2♣. Voila!

Danny much prefers to pass, retaining 1NT as a Sternberg Transfer to 2♣. Danny wonders: what would the doubler do if you didn't have a scrambling 1NT available, or chose not to make one?

THE STRIPED-TAIL APE

Sometimes you just can't trust your shifty-eyed opponents. Every once in a while, this situation raises its ugly tail, er---we mean head.

In some auctions, an opponent may suspect that you are about to bid a slam that he can't beat. So just when you are about to try for slam over your partner's game bid, your right-hand opponent doubles. Trying to keep from drooling, you pass.

But you can't keep from drooling when you make 4♠ doubled with three overtricks on routine play and enter +1390 on the traveling scoresheet. Your drool turns to tears when you see the ten +1460's and two +2210's scored at other tables. Yes, all your counterparts bid and made slams.

The late John Lowenthal reported that he and a friend visited the Amazon jungle, where the natives employed this strategy regularly.

As John and his partner debated which of them should have redoubled, the perpetrator explained, "Then we run from redouble---zoom, like striped-tail ape."

We have our doubts about John's geology and zoology. Is the habitat of the Striped-Tail Ape really the Amazon jungle, or is it Madagascar? And was the perpetrator of the clever ploy a striped-tail ape, or was he an oversized lemur?

Here is an example. You are vul versus non-vulnerable opponents.

You	Lefty	Partner	Righty
1♦	2♠	3♠	4♠
4NT	P	5♦	Dbl
?			

Now what? You were going bid 6♦. Does Righty have a real penalty double, perhaps a trump stack? Or is he a Striped-Tail Ape? If you pass and take 12 tricks, you will score plus 950 losing to everyone who bid 6♦ for 1370. If you redouble, RHO will run to 5♠, perhaps down five, minus 1100.

How can you tell what kind of double he has made? You might do well to ask him to stand up so you could check his anatomy. Very diabolical.

Deal # 19   Fantasy or Swindle?

At favorable vulnerability, non-vul versus vul, your partner opens 4♡ in first seat and your RHO bids 4♠.

You hold: ♠ 862 ♡ Q8765 ◊109 ♣ 762.

What are your options? How many hearts should you bid? You are certainly not passing. Any other ideas?

How about a penalty double? "Have you two lost your minds?" you may wonder. "How do you expect to beat 4♠?"

No, we haven't lost our minds, just stretched them a bit. What do you think the opponents can make? A small slam? A grand? They certainly are going to bid 6♠.and score at least 1430. If they make 4♠ doubled, they score 790 plus 200 for each overtrick, total 1190 or 1390.

What will they bid over your double? That's their problem, not yours. But if either opponent redoubles, don't be stubborn. High-tail it back to five hearts, just like they do in Brazil---er, Madagascar.

```
                        ♠ 9
                        ♡ A K J 10 9 3 2
                        ◊ J 8 5 4
                        ♣ 9
        ♠ K J 5                         ♠ A Q 10 7 4 3
        ♡ void                          ♡ 4
        ◊ A K 7 3 2                     ◊ Q 6
        ♣ K Q 8 4 3                     ♣ A J 10 5
                        ♠ 8 6 2
                        ♡ Q 8 7 6 5
                        ◊ 10 9
                        ♣ 7 6 2
```

CHAPTER

FIFTEEN

ADDITIONAL

DEALS 20 – 32

Deal # 20   Defending by Counting Declarer's Tricks

North
♠ K 9 6
♡ 8 5 3 2
♢ Q J 10 7
♣ A 4

West
♠ 5 2
♡ A Q 7
♢ A K 5
♣ K Q 8 7 3

South	West	North	East
1♠	Dbl	Redbl	2♣
2♠	3♣	3♠	P
4♠	All Pass		

Opening Lead: ♢A

After West's takeout double, North deemed his hand a bit too good for a simple raise. He started with a redouble, planning on bidding 2♠ later.

Note East's 2♣ bid. Does it show any particular length and strength? Yes.

East's 2♣ shows 0 HCP (minimum) to 1 HCP (maximum). That's what the auction marks him with. And he promises at least four clubs.

After East follows with the ♢2 at Trick 1, West switches to the ♣K. Declarer wins dummy's ♣A and ruffs dummy's last club. He cashes the ♠Q and ♠J as East follows and leads the ♢8 to West's ♢K. How should West continue?

Don't panic! Declarer can take six spades, one club, and two diamonds. That's nine tricks. He needs a heart for his tenth. By waiting patiently with his ♡AQ and exiting passively in diamonds, West will get the two heart tricks he needs to beat 4♠ before South gets one heart trick. Down one.

East
♠ 7 3
♡ 9 6
♢ 9 6 4 2
♣ J 9 6 5 2

South
♠ A Q J 10 8 4
♡ K J 10 4
♢ 8 3
♣ 10

Deal # 21   Doubler Beware

You open 2NT on ♠ K97 ♡ QJ ◇ KQ4 ♣ AKQJ7.   Then you face:

South	West	North	East
2NT	3♡	P	4♡
?			

No respect. Don't they know you have 21 points? Will you let them escape undoubled? So you double and West redoubles. The nerve!

But which four tricks do you expect to take? The two heart quacks that will fall beneath the ♡A and ♡K? The ♠K? Where do you think the ♠A is? Three top clubs? Do you really expect declarer and dummy each to have three? You'll be lucky if two of them cash. The ◇KQ? Yes, a likely trick here.

```
                    ♠ 10 6 5 4
                    ♡ void
                    ◇ J 6 5 3 2
                    ♣ 9 6 4 2
  ♠ A J 8 2                         ♠ Q 3
  ♡ A 10 9 8 7 4 3                  ♡ K 6 5 2
  ◇ 10 8                            ◇ A 9 7
  ♣ Void                            ♣ 10 8 5 3
                    ♠ K 9 7
                    ♡ Q J
                    ◇ K Q 4
                    ♣ A K Q J 7
```

Very nice! You open 2NT and they can make a slam. 4♠ redoubled, making six. That's minus 1480 instead of minus 480. A lot of IMP's to explain to your teammates. And had they been vul, minus 2280!

To add insult to injury, your partner says, "Don't you know that when you double like a Striped-Tail Ape, you must be prepared to flee like one? You had nowhere to go."

Beware of doubling with just shmoints as Danny called them long before Marty Bergen did. You need tricks, usually trump tricks.

Deal # 22   More Annoying Preempts

Vul E/W

```
                    ♠ 10 9 2
                    ♡ 9 4
                    ◊ 4 2
                    ♣ Q J 8 7 5 4
    ♠ A J 7                          ♠ K Q 8 6 4 3
    ♡ A Q 8 2                        ♡ K 10 5
    ◊ 10 8 7 6 5                     ◊ K J
    ♣ K                              ♣ 3 2
                    ♠ 5
                    ♡ J 7 6 3
                    ◊ A Q 9 3
                    ♣ A 10 9 6
```

East	South	West	North
1♠	Dbl	Redbl	3♣
P	5♣	?	

After South doubled, West redoubled, planning to show a game-forcing hand with three-card spade support.

South bid 5♣, not expecting to make it but knowing North had no defensive values, wanted to exert maximum pressure.

What should West do? Even if now his ♣K is wasted, he still has a game-going hand with good three-card spade support, but should he bid 5♠?

As the cards lie East can likely make 5♠, as North cannot get in to lead diamonds, and declarer can pick up the hearts to discard a diamond.

West's redouble was fine. Just another case of those annoying preempts.

So what should West do? Why not pass and let East decide whether to double or take the push?

A pass by West here implies three-card support for East's major.

Deal # 23   Running From a Double

As South you pick up your usual ♠ J5 ♡ 973 ♢ 543 ♣ 109764, and partner opens a 15-17 1NT. Your RHO doubles: penalty, in the absence of an alert.

Not good. Where shall you run?

It's more important than ever to have opener, the strong hand, declare. You want the opening lead to come from the doubler's strength up to opener's strength instead of through opener, So all actions by responder should be transfers, including a redouble. Playing in your five-card suit will usually be better.

Here are some simple agreements:

Pass – I'm content to let you play in 1NT doubled. If you have a maximum, you may make an overtrick. Or I have nowhere to run.

Redouble ('reclubble') to show clubs. 2♣ shows diamonds. 2♢ shows hearts. 2♡ shows spades.

These are the basics. If this is your only partnership agreement, it will be reasonably adequate, and any further calls will be just as you play them after ordinary Jacoby Transfers.

There are fancier schemes. If your partner is up to it, you can play *Kobe* (described earlier), but don't twist his arm to do so. Memory burden can outweigh technical advantages.

Deal # 24   Who's Vulnerable?

```
Dealer South      ♠ J 9 5
Vul: Choose       ♡ K J 10 9 2
                  ◊ J 10
                  ♣ A K 10
♠ Q 4                                    ♠ 6 3 2
♡ A Q 6 4                                ♡ 5 3
◊ K Q 9                                  ◊ 7 5 2
♣ Q J 6 3                                ♣ 9 8 5 4 2
                  ♠ A K 10 8 7
                  ♡ 8 7
                  ◊ A 8 6 4 3
                  ♣ 7
```

South opens 1♠. Should West make a takeout double? Let's start with E/W vul, N/S non-vul. It's a marginal double, the ♠Q may be worthless and doubling over spades forces partner to reply at the two-level, so you need a bit extra.

North redoubles; he has a game force with three-card spade support. Not playing Sternberg Transfers, East bids 2♣, the only suit he can stand. Should South bid in front of North?

We think so. Despite South's 3 Honor Tricks, North might have ◊ KQxx and find that it's worthless on defense. South's 2◊ bid will tell him so.

Should West raise clubs? East has promised no values. To bid 3♣ would invite disaster---even in the absence of North's redouble. Count the losers in a club contract. Two spades, three clubs, one in each red suit. Down three doubled, -800.

The numbers will be different at equal vulnerability, but 3♣ doubled will still cost more than the value of a North-South game.

Finally, look at the deal with North-South vul and East-West not. Will North double 3♣ if West bids it? We think not. The 500-point penalty won't compensate for the missed vulnerable game.

But that does not mean West *should* bid 3♣ on favorable vulnerability. For he cannot assume that North and South can bid and make a game. What if the best they can do is bid and make a partscore? Then even minus 300 will be disastrous.

Deal # 25   Foolishness

As South, you hold ♠ KQ9742 ♡ 872 ◇ A ♣ KQ9. East deals and opens a Weak 2♡ Bid in front of you. You overcall 2♠ and the auction continues:

West	North	East	South
		2♡	2♠
3♡	4♡	Dbl	P
P	Redbl	P	?

What do you make of North's redouble? How should you continue?

Had East passed over 4♡, what would you have bid? 4♠?

Partner's 4♡ cue-bid was a try for a spade slam, but as his only clear slam try below game, it did not promise anything more specific. His redouble clarified, promising first-round control, often the ♡A but perhaps a void---and surely a void when East doubled 4♡.

If you play Roman Keycard Blackwood, you may have feared to invoke it as you might have two heart losers off the top. East may have opened a Weak 2♡ with a strong five-bagger, or West may have raised on a high doubleton honor. But now your heart worries are assuaged.

East's double wasn't very smart. We suppose he bid it to remind West that he had indeed opened a Weak 2♡ Bid. But it helped you, giving your partner an extra turn to show first-round heart control. Now you can bid 4NT as RKB *excluding the ♡A.*

```
                    ♠ A 8 6 3
                    ♡ void
                    ◇ Q J 10
                    ♣ A 8 6 5 4 3
   ♠ J                              ♠ 10 5
   ♡ K J 6 4                        ♡ A Q 10 9 5 3
   ◇ 9 7 5 4 3                      ◇ K 8 6 2
   ♣ J 10 2                         ♣ 7
```

"Gee, thanks," said West, as he marked -2210 on his private score. "Without your double, I would never have guessed to lead a heart against four spades."

As West holding ♠ KQJ ♡ 974 ◊ 109732 ♣ 62 in a team game, you sit quietly while North opens 1♡ as dealer and the opponents bid to 6♠ unopposed.

1♡	1♠	
3♠	4NT*	*Roman Keycard Blackwood
5♣**	6♠	**three keys

Do you think South can make 6♠? Obviously not, unless East is Sharon Sharptung, who led a club against 7♠ and revoked before Danny could score his ♠A in a rubber bridge game forty years ago. Danny remembers the post-mortem:

"You had the ace of trump and you didn't double?" asked Sharon as Danny wrote 2210 on the *They* side of the scoresheet and totaled the score for the rubber.

"A double would have been Lightner," answered Danny. "I was afraid you'd lead diamonds, dummy's first-bid suit."

Did you double 6♠? *Should* you have doubled? Suppose you doubled and South fled to 6NT. Would you double again and lead the ♠K?

If you double again South redoubles. "Greedy!" chides North, but South only grins.

When you compare scores, your South teammate apologizes: "Sorry, minus 50. We bid 6♠ but trumps split three-zero. And you?" Hmmm, minus 1660.

When opponents bid strongly to a slam, they're unlikely to fail by much. Yes, had they passed 6♠ doubled, you'd have scored +100 instead of plus +50. You'd have gained 2 IMPs. Hmmm. Win 2 or lose 17? Not very good odds.

South	North
♠ A 10 7 4 3 2	♠ 9 8 6 5
♡ 3	♡ A K Q J 10
◊ A Q	◊ K J
♣ A Q J 10	♣ K 8

Deal # 27   Another Whoops

Vul Both   As West you see this auction:

	West	North	East	South	
West				1♠	
♠ A Q 10 9					
♡ 10 6	P	2♣*	P	2♡	*game-forcing
◊ Q J 8	P	2♠	P	4♠	
♣ K J 9 3	?				

Looking at four likely trump tricks, should you double? How will you feel when South 'sends it back'?

By doubling, you told the greedy South who redoubled that you had a trump stack.

```
                      ♠ 8 5 2
                      ♡ Q 3
                      ◊ A K 3
                      ♣ A 10 7 5 2
   ♠ A Q 10 9                        ♠ 6
   ♡ 10 6                            ♡ J 9 8 4
   ◊ Q J 8                           ◊ 10 9 7 6 5
   ♣ K J 9 3                         ♣ Q 8 4
                      ♠ K J 7 4 3
                      ♡ A K 7 5 2
                      ◊ 4 2
                      ♣ 6
```

West led the ◊Q to dummy's ◊K. Warned by the double, South didn't touch trumps. He took the ♣A, ruffed a club, led to dummy's ◊A and ruffed another club. He cashed the ♡A, led to dummy's ♡Q and ruffed dummy's last diamond.

Having won eight tricks, he led the ♡K. West ruffed with the ♠9 and led the ♠A and ♠10. South won and led another heart. Dummy's ♠8 was going to be the tenth trick.

E/W minus 1080.

The worst penalty doubles are those that tell declarer how to play the hand. If undoubled he might have failed. And when they send it back redoubled?

Deal # 28   Using Their Doubles

```
              ♠ K J 9 6 4 3            West    North    East    South
              ♡ A 10 3 2                                         1♠
              ◊ 7 5 3                   P      4♣*      Dbl     4◊
              ♣ Void                    Dbl    4♡       Dbl     Redbl
♠ void                  ♠ 7 2           P      5♣       Dbl     6♠
♡ 9 6 5 4               ♡ K Q J 8
◊ Q 10 9 8 2            ◊ K 6 4              All Pass
♣ K 8 4 3              ♣ A J 10 9
              ♠ A Q 10 8 5              *ambiguous splinter
              ♡ 7                        (singleton or void)
              ◊ A J
              ♣ Q 7 6 5 2
```

What do you think of that auction? A lot of noise. Do you think East's three doubles helped his side or his opponents? What about South's redouble?

Doubling a splinter bid for a lead of that suit usually helps declarer more than the defense. There are better uses for splinter doubles. Doubling 4◊ made no sense, as West had mediocre diamonds and was going to be on lead.

East's double of 4♡ gave South a chance to make his only useful call, a redouble to show second-round control. That gave North and South the extra bidding space they needed to reach 6♠.

In the 1990s, Danny wrote a *Bridge World* article advocating using doubles of splinters to ask partner to lead the highest-ranking suit other than that suit and the trump suit. Many pairs have adopted that use. Danny now has a slightly different idea. Use a double of a splinter to suggest sacrificing in that suit but only if it's higher-ranking than the splinterer's intended trump suit. If it's lower-ranking, a double still asks for the lead of the highest-ranking unbid suit

As played by most, splinters are ambiguous, showing either singletons or voids. Opinion about splintering with singleton aces is divided, some say yes, some say no. Doubling a splinter is *anti-preemptive*, as gives both opponents an extra option, a chance to show *void or ace* by redoubling, and lets Lefty pass to give Righty a chance to clarify.

♠ Q 10 9 2
♡ A K 10
◊ K Q J 2
♣ A 4

♠ 3
♡ Q J 8 7 5 3 2
◊ 10 8 5
♣ Q 5

♠ A 6 5 4
♡ 6
◊ 9 4 3
♣ 10 9 8 3 2

♠ K J 8 7
♡ 9 4
◊ A 7 6
♣ K J 7 6

From a team game at the 2021 United States Bridge Federation Open Trials USA-2 final. At one table North opened 1◊ and raised South's 1♠ bid to 4♠ ending the auction, the opponents silent. South won the opening heart lead and drew two rounds of trumps, East ducking. When declarer began cashing top hearts, East ruffed the second, and could only take one more trick, his ♠A. Making five, +650.

Why did his team lose 13 IMPs?

In the other room, North liked his strong spot-cards in the majors enough to scrape up a 2NT opening. After North replied 3♠ to South's Stayman 3♣. South used a conventional 4♡ rebid (called *OMAR* for *Other Major Relays or also The Impossible Major*) to suggest slam in spades.

West doubled. Did he think a heart lead against a spade slam would be helpful? North redoubled to show the ♡A. Thus encouraged, South checked for keycards via Roman Keycard Blackwood and put North in 6♠.

East's heart lead didn't help his side. North won the opening heart lead and played two rounds of trumps, ducked as at the other table. Confident that West had the remaining heart honor, North led a third spade. East won the ♠A and exited with his last spade. When declarer cashed top winners in the minors and the ♣Q fell doubleton, he didn't even need to finesse the ♡10 to make 6♠, +1430 and 13 IMPs.

West's double allowing North to redouble helped the opponents in the bidding and the play.

```
                            ♠ 7 6
                            ♡ K Q J 8
                            ◊ K 10 9
                            ♣ K Q 4 2
        ♠ Q 10 2                              ♠ K 5 4 3
        ♡ 10 7 6 2                            ♡ A 3
        ◊ 8 6                                 ◊ Q 4 2
        ♣ 10 6 5 3                            ♣ A J 9 8
                            ♠ A J 9 8
                            ♡ 9 5 4
                            ◊ A J 7 5 3
                            ♣ 7
```

Another deal from the same event featured light 1◊ openings at both tables on favorable vulnerability. Would you have opened? We wouldn't.

The auction proceeded similarly until South's third turn:

West	North	East	South	
			1◊	
P	1♡	Dbl	Redbl*	*Support Redouble (three hearts)
P	P	1♠	?	

At one table, South passed, letting East off the hook. When 1♠ came round to him, North cue-bid 2♠ and reached 3NT, down one on a misguess of the ◊Q, minus 50.

At the other table, South, having four spades and probably thinking his two jacks were extras, doubled 1♠. North, having about three kings more than he might have had for his 1♡ response, sat for the double, as did everyone else.

North overtook South's ♡9 opening lead with the ♡J, which held. He shifted to the ♠7, which rode to dummy's ♠10. Declarer led to the ♣Q and ♣A, then low to dummy's ♠Q. North won the next club with the ♣K as South discarded a heart.

Now a diamond shift put South in to cash the ♠A. Continued diamond leads held declarer to three trump tricks and two side aces, down two, minus 500.

117

Deal # 31   Decision Time

You, South, hold ♠ AKQ ♡ J72 ◊ AQJ7 ♣ 532 and face:

West	North	East	South
1♡	2♣	P	?

You feel some pity for East, who probably has a yarborough, but then you realize that he might as many as 2 or 3 HCP. For West may have opened on 10 or 11 HCP with Honor Tricks and shape, while North may have only 10 HCP for his two-level overcall.

For lack of any other reasonable way to force, you cue-bid 2♡. Maybe you can reach 3NT, the most likely-seeming game if partner has a heart stopper. Even a partial stopper, a singleton or doubleton ♡K or ♡Q, will do. By your next turn …

West	North	East	South	
1♡	2♣	P	2♡*	* good hand
Dbl**	P	P	?	** "Didn't you hear me open one heart?"

What now? The actual South redoubled. What kind of redouble was that?

Nobody knows. It wasn't SOS, as South's 2♡ wasn't natural. It wasn't a cue-bid redouble, as it wasn't based on the ♡A. It fetched 2♠ from North.

South might have bid a timid 3♣ and let North play there. Or he might have brazened it out in 3NT, our choice, hoping to catch North with a partial stopper and offering the most to gain if successful. Either would make. Sometimes you just have to guess.

South bid 3◊. He caught North with a minimum overcall, a singleton ◊10, and nowhere to go. 3◊ went down one. East had a singleton too, the ♡Q.

Notice that at no point in this auction did South make a bid that showed what kind of hand he had. Contrary to popular belief, neither cue-bids nor redoubles are a panacea.

Deal # 32   Do You See the Stripes on the Tail of the Ape?

Jim had a surprise 8-hour layover in Los Angeles Monday morning on his recent trip to Japan. He called Danny from the airport and asked,
"Are you available for a session of duplicate bridge today?"

"We're in luck, Jim," said Danny. "Fifi just canceled. Hop in a cab right away 'cause the game starts at 10:30. Beverly Hills Bridge Club on
La Cienega between Olympic Boulevard and Gregory Way."

When Jim arrived at 10:17, Danny thrust a convention card in front of him. Jim saw "D. Kleinman – F. Guggenheim" at the top and asked,
"Any relation to the infamous Mrs.---"

"Yes," interrupted Danny. "The dear lady was Fifi's grandmother."

Jim looked askance at some of the conventions on Fifi's card but this was no time to make changes. This was the second board of the third round:

	♠ J 8 3		E-W vul			
	♥ J 3		West	North	East	South
	♦ Q J 10 8 3 2				1NT*	2♦**
Jim	♣ Q 2	Danny	2NT***	P	3♣	5♥
♠ Q 6		♠ 9 5	P	5♠	Dbl	6♥
♥ 5		♥ A 10 7	P	P	Dbl	All Pass
♦ 7 6 5 4		♦ A K 9				
♣ A J 6 5 4 3		♣ K 10 9 8 7				
	Wily Willie		*16-18 HCP			
	♠ A K 10 7 4 2		**Hamilton (majors)			
	♥ K Q 9 8 6 4 2		***Lebensohl			
	♦ void					
	♣ void					

Jim led the ♣A. Danny encouraged with the ♣10. Willie ruffed and led the ♥K. Danny won the ♥A and continued the ♣K. Willie ruffed and Jim dropped the ♣J.

"Signals?" asked Willie.

"We play Congratulory Jacks," said Danny, naming a convention devised by David Weiss.

Willie counted the points. He looked at Jim's convention card and saw the old-fashioned 16-18 HCP range. With Jim having shown up with ♣AJ, Danny needed all the remaining high cards for his 1NT.

"I play *Entry Jacks*," said Willie, After cashing the ♠A, he crossed to dummy's ♥J, and let dummy's ♠J ride. Oops, down one.

"Another success for the Striped-Tail Ape Double," said Danny.

"Not so fast, Danny," said Willie. He called the director and complained, "Danny opened a 14-point notrump but Jim announced '16 to 18.' And then Jim failed to alert Danny's Striped-Tail Ape Double."

The director shook his finger at Jim. "Shame on you! You should have announced '14 to 19'---or whatever your range actually is. The Striped-Tail Ape is still on the Endangered Species List, so you must alert him. Just this once, I'll let you get away with it, but don't you do it again."

Then, shaking another finger. "And you, Danny: take that nasty Australopithecine back to the zoo where he belongs."

Well, dear reader: do you think the director acted fairly?

Printed in the United States
by Baker & Taylor Publisher Services